Other titles by Arthur Weil:

Illusion Diffusion
Word Shots
Eat My Words
Dare-Devilish and Divine
Have Fun While You Can
Words to Fly With
Life, Love and Gems That Shine
Exploding Mind (or 'Not Over the Hill Yet')
Poetry is for Sissies
Reflections of the Moment
The Fluid Word
Slice of Life
Theater of Thoughts
Love Always
Liquid Words
Not Shakespeare, Just Me
Wacky and Wonderful, Wireless Words
Word Missiles, Here and Now

Please visit me at my website

www.poetrypearls.com

I am greatly thankful to my editor and book designer
Alison Clarke Bodden
for her invaluable help in bringing this "Best Of" poetry book to print.
Without her it would not have come to fruition.
For that, I am hugely grateful.
AW

Table of Contents

A Mental Meal

of Magical

Rhymes and Poems

The Very Best of Arthur Weil
Volume 1

A Mental Meal

of Magical Rhymes and Poems

For all inquiries or to order additional copies of his books at discounted prices, contact Arthur Weil, 208 Pala Avenue, Piedmont, CA 94611, by email at: aweil444@aol.com or go to www.poetrypearls.com.

These books make excellent gifts and are all personally signed by the author.

Pricing is $14.95 per copy.

ISBN: 978-097884568-1
Printed in the USA by United Graphics Incorporated

A Brief Introduction

Congratulations!

Words here, there and everywhere I share; to **stimulate**, *to encourage you to think, to doubt and even to cuss!*

Please do not attempt to read this book in one fell swoop. That would be **torture!**

Rather, absorb a few pages here and there, as appetizers to savor; a treasure trove to be discovered. You'll find rhymes and expressions, some clever, trite, intuitive, stimulating, and sometimes even boring!

Don't try to figure me out. Even I haven't been able to do that myself, and I am 88 years young. So please, please just a few pages at a time. You might even get an inkling to revolutionize the world with your own words. It needs it, you know. And please, never forget to give love, lots of it. Embraces, hugs and smiles are OK too.

This book embodies my creed, "I love you, man. I love you, woman!"

Yes, I love life.

*Go to it. Eat a few pages...
...but beware, they may bite back.*

chapter one: today/here and now

Here And Now

"Here and Now" is your life at this very moment in space and time.

Your Here and Now is this instant, as you read this book – your own Here and Now. In more philosophical terms; by the time you reach the "Here and Now" consciously, it is already fleetingly gone, for better or for worse. Yet you and I live a lifetime of "Here and Now"; be it great, fantastic or sometimes humanly disappointing.

As with all of our life, what we do with our "Here and Now" is easier said than done. You could eat a delicious green salad with cucumbers, tomatoes, nuts and very light dressing to enrich your body, satisfy your hunger. Or you could choose to eat a fast-food meal with no nutritional value. You make conscious decisions in what you do every minute of your day. You could hug your girlfriend/boyfriend or husband/wife, friends, children; shower them with kisses, and declare your love and friendship over and over again. Or maybe you can visit a charity; feed the homeless, read to patients, tutor in schools.

All of these enrich your life, your spirit and your humanity.

Or maybe you can just simply put on your PJs and catch up on necessary sleep ready for the next day.

"Here and Now" can be a spiritual, uplifting experience, either at home or at a gathering, as you contemplate and appreciate that good times have come to stay. You have so much choice in the here and now. If still puzzled, get a good book or magazine, escape to a movie with friends, go to the gym, or even munch on carrots and fresh fruit. I personally like apples, pears, raspberries and strawberries.

But I like mostly to be with a friend, in my "Here and Now".

In short, "Here and Now" is where you start the rest of your life. It's yours! Take time out – plan – and dare act!

Amazing Day

There isn't a silent second
That adds up to
A silent minute
Which adds up to be a noisy hour
And a fantastic, symphonic
Colorful
Spectacular day

The soundless second hand glides
Into the hours of my day
Momentous, stupendous, marvelous
Disastrous, painful, surviving
Like the clock
My silent heart thumps
To the rhythm of our revolving earth

All to return
To the still blackness
Of the timeless night

"Here and Now", Art Weil 2012

Airing Out

I fling open the window
To let the cool, clean air in
Or the stifling, stale air out

Sometimes the brisk draft is uncomfortable
Depending on which way the wind blows
I squirm, I smile, I grimace

Each breeze against my skin
Inhale the stagnant
Or celebrate the freshness

It's Nature, sloughing off dust
Fumes, chemicals transferring
My atmosphere – my life

I keep the window open
Like a stern soldier warding off evil
I cherish my existence

For me to inhale warm or cool –
Breezy – rustling or in silence
Can't you feel the change in the air?

You, I, we – simply, automatically breathe
Who has time to analyze the gasses?
Amazing – the power of air and water!

Just a little penetrating draft and
Our perception and thought soon modified
I know I can't keep the window open forever

≈ ≈ ≈

I welcome the day
The day doesn't always welcome me

Ringling Bros Circus, New York

Blithe Spirit

Blithe spirit travels on the sunbeam
On ten thousand dust particles
Transports to a mysterious destination
Open mouth - inhales
Enraptured, captured by the spirit "Why now - why me?"
He happily acknowledges
Today fate is my bride I shall tarry, romp and ride
The joyous overtones of merriment
Accolades heaved, success granted
Feverish, he decides, almost concurs
Was it all perception, or reality?
Its stamp is tough and lasting
Computer space awarded, the victor
With open arms he/she is received
Believes until the battery dies down
Then the silent shadow vanishes with the sinking sun.

The Day

The day was fraught with improprieties
Strung as intermissions
Wrong clothes
Wrong words
Wrong chewing
Toothpick, fingers
Wrong flowers and gifts
The awkward etiquette
Of a civilized society
That knows how to kiss

But there's always tomorrow

Evening Reflection to Sunny Morn

Bombard me with the visual prospect
Silhouette of shapely maiden
Magnificent posture reflected in the mirrored lake
So many dreamt, but she has won
Received the lucky lottery prize
A thousand confirmations of the young
Seeing is not always believing
Like the bubbly beer foam
Like the rain-soaked evening clouds
That melts by morning with the beaming sun
Like the last echo in the hills
All so susceptible to disappear
And dissipate so quickly
Leaving but a brief memory
Left is space, and brook, green valleys
Birds chirp, the rustling branches, some echoes
Visible and audible, I don't give a damn
As the blazing sun sparkles again
And we all dance, gyrate, join and jump
Into the fray of day

14

AWAKENING

Felicitations - greetings
To the Globe
Whose ice cap melts
Yet billions, aware of catastrophe
Are helpless and on the move
Each nation selfishly protective
Will Armageddon shower down
As we eke out a living or
Relish in the new wealth of inventions?

We are intelligent - but like a blind man
Ignore it - it's not happening to us...
Leaders can just do so much, but you?
Awake America.
Awake World.
There is a new dark devilish dawn
Can our posterity be saved in time?

∿ ∿ ∿

A blank page can be easily filled by creative words
A blank day is yours to fill wisely
A blank lifetime never exists

My Shower Is Waiting

Before my shower
Naked and vulnerable
Yet proud, relaxed, free
Not much I can do about me!
Somehow routine, with wash cloth
From face, neck all over
While hot water and soap pour over me
We all live only in one body
Mine - unique, special, now
Not lean anymore
Bit misshapen
Sit or stand - stark naked I can accept me
Do I have a choice ?
Head unwieldy I am most comfortable unclothed
I smile
The shower is always great
Good riddance – refreshed – ready to go!
Imagine, a new day has just begun

≈ ≈ ≈

Many of us are so sophisticated
That we don't know front from end
or where the true middle is.

The gray cold dust on a dirty morning
can end up as a pleasant golden sunshine
with a pink sunset at dusk

Kiss

A kiss that lasts ten seconds
Kiss them goodbye
Never to applaud
Torment or ridicule
Taste the palate
Half blinded by the ecstasy
Feel the sensation
Spontaneous thrill
What are you thinking now?
Too late?
Each second more precious
Ah, the rapture lingers on
Time is my nemesis
Encapsulate and use it wisely
Because a kiss passes us by
Never to return

≈ ≈ ≈

It isn't fair
And I don't care
What nerve
When life throws you a curve

A little hanky-panky, a little romance
Life always gives us another chance

Another Chance

Can I be there for you?
Can you be there for me,
To give, to share
And to be true?
Can we create a lasting friendship
And be born anew?

Early Morning

Early morning, mysterious quiet
As if a suspended corpse shows life
Twilight innocently rushed
What if the dead one is really not – not yet
One limb shows sign of movement
What about the pale, ashen face?
Golden search for sun's scenario
Only last night the radio blared:
Car sped, daring twenty-two year old
The early morn is the slow first movement of a symphony
Body on the stretcher visibly alive
Are there not two eyes and ears sensitive to the aura in the room?
Outside, another morn breaks
Blooming rose petals opening, aroma
The limp body has no bloody contusion
Nor split bowels

But the silent cry of a hit-run victim
A white-gowned nurse is entering the room
Will there be time to save the victim?
Before the sunshine sucks energy
Displaced with a billion rays
Announces the inevitable morning

And mercifully robs the coroner
Of another forensic inspection

Empty Mind

The empty mind
Never!
Latent, yes...
Filled, like a glass of water
Invisible, weighty liquid
Replete with miniscule computer chips
World's most impressive gift
Refilled all the nerve endings
Reacted most powerfully
First chemical reaction:
Stimulated
Then
All hell broke loose

chapter two: funky people

Our open-minded youth today accepts the zest of Funky People. Generations ago I, you, all of us could have had that label. So wonderful to see fresh souls rap and express their happy lives. Funky, fun and carefree spells youth, spells newness, a daring, different, new generation.

They are the innocent aberrations that make for positive change. You probably were one of the shakers and movers of your time. They, the young, new generation are the new protagonists, the new revolutionaries who demand fairness and participation, not always readily accepted as they push the extremes. Yet their freshness, newly liberated, is neither right nor wrong. Their raucous or sentimental songs ring true. Their poetry and lyrics of life may be in your face. Sometimes disheveled, careless, funky, free, dressed in every type of garb. They are the new Funky People.

They stop the traffic in the street. They invent their own idioms in our language. With homemade signs, they parade and protest, indifferent to the risks of protest. They lay their bodies on the line to protest an injustice. They oppose war, and their voices reverberate loudly.

They were the flower children or street people of the 60's; often educated, but sometimes living in apparent poverty. They dared, took chances. In time we took notice, even if we disagreed, criticized their dress, their radicalism, their strategy and looks. Some dropped out of school, lived in communes, or simply congregated in cities. Attached to their dogs, they were a polyglot of many persuasions: hippy, agnostic, atheist, radical. But when it came to discrimination and injustice, they spoke as one voice.

Looking back on the "radicals" of two generations ago, they look tame to us today, as this era's Funky People modernize our way of life and change the values of life today.

For each new generation is a wake-up call. They infuse new blood, new visions and sometimes, sometimes touch us with their eagerness. You and I, we were part of bringing the young generation to where they are now. Thank God they exist today. This is what makes our country so great, so unique.

Hurrah for Funky People!

Funky People

Foolish, frivolous, full of zest
Fallaciously showering accolades
Fortunately, figuratively speaking few survive
Few meet the test
A little funkiness enriches,
Makes us smile, out of the way
Too much, too much – furtive and frolic
Fervently we must escape the fragmented mile
Find fantastic fun filled figurines in style
For a few mementoes foolishly flirt
A funky fantasy to tune of willow bird
Return to fallacy of fatal fumigated form
So dull, so factual, so norm

Gay Pride Parade, San Francisco 2012

Who Am I anyhow? Who are we anyhow?

If found I am not what
I said I am
Shining example of goodness
Under whose thin skin
Lurks envy, deception
A righteous risk, deal dangerous

Consumptive, self-involved
"You say I am honest?"
Innocently peer at my neighbor's cards
Intuitively steal looks at all the pretty gals
Who among us is so honest
To pray forgiveness the next day?

Are all many-sided, complicated creatures
All with great ego
A mystic shadow of temptation, ambivalence
In an instant the mind turns
One hundred and eighty degrees
Opinions modified, strong outbursts rationalized
My way most, yours - a bit here and there
Anxious protect our own
No, but spirited, overwhelmed
With mischievous passion to subdue the maiden

I am not what I said I am
Sometimes I am not myself
Devout, intense, pray to my deity
My competitiveness makes for action
Forcefully winning, succeeding
My meditation brings some balance and reason
One thing is for sure
I do not want to be a slave to
Anyone

Spaced Out

Old friend turned weird and wild
Radical judgment, most disturbing sight
How can I communicate?
He acted most peculiar of late
I love him, learned, earned friend
Miscommunication at the end
Now he's on self-destruct
As if from crazy house now plucked

I'm a helpless observer, sense his pain
Why do so many go insane?
He left his wife, his children he ignored
Friends run away, feel violated, often bored
He's stubborn, yet his own inviolate man
No rhyme nor reason, has no plan

His weird charade will do him in
Once he was respected, oh, what sin
Now by most much neglected
Drinks, pills, depression simply wrecked it
In isolation, session after session,
"Get yourself together, go to some confession
Pray you will recover, be okay!"
Far-fetched see the light of day

For only he can stop and resurrect
Blame it on life, on pressure and too much neglect
Psychiatrist and doctor's medicine in store
New attitude and scenery by self will do far more
It's difficult from darkness to climb to light
Hope, like others who succeeded in this fight
Institutions may give some might
Better than unnecessary funerals, that's right

Rattle

There are the crazies, the lazies
The cuties, the booties
Incessant so present
Extreme sane so inane
The artist, the not missed
That's most of us kissed

Gala with rubies and rings
Studded diamonds for kings
The foreign, the natives
The copiers, the creatives
It's the lot
A stew in a pot
Few prizes some realize
Ideas on the rise

Joy is our treasure
Study at our leisure
Delightful, delicate, feast
Calmed, quartered the beast
Nothing is taken
Nothing forsaken

≈ ≈ ≈

Obsessive people are hard to bear
Some brainy, most full of hot air
And if to please them, let them score
They simply ask for more

Mr. Good and Mrs. Mean

Mr. Good and Mrs. Mean
Decided to go to a party.
Compliments on the event by Mr. Good
Snide remarks from Mrs. Mean
"You don't know anything," she exhorted
"Maybe I don't," Mr. Good said,
"But I sure enjoy helping people, caring and giving."
"Poppycock," rattled Mrs. Mean,
"Why help? They don't deserve it."
Soon a little girl came with auburn hair, ponytails
and a great big smile.
"Would you like some cookies?" she asked
as she held the plate graciously.
"Oh, thank you, yes," Mr. Good retorted.
"Go away little girl," Mrs. Mean said
In an unfriendly manner and turned away.

And so they lived unhappily ever after.

I Would Judge

Addicted to late night
TV
I binge to escape from
me
Absorbed in visual
inane
If I were outside of me
I would judge such a
person insane
Or certainly in need of
help

We hugged

We hugged - that's all
In our pajamas sometime around 3 or 4 am
We hugged - that's all
Our warm bodies pressed the seconds into hours
Then back to sleep again
It was a deep, strong
Commitment by two loving people
One of them was me
We hugged - that's all

Guilt

Each of us carries a hidden
Invisible weight of guilt
In each step – intentional or not –
That with each hour of joy
Yet moral creatures dream of wrong
A long ago foolish, innocent act
Happiness as an ankle chain draws us down
It is the imperfection of our life, our world
As we stoop and straighten a bit with
    Effort
        Good deed
           Creation
           And
                Move
                    On...

The steep staircase of life's learning
Straight, then crooked, curved,
Circular, ever endlessly upward
On this sensational, scenic trip of lusty life
Vast panoramas, pictorial, pleasing eyes and palate, influenced,
tutored, loved, cajoled by many
All eyes on the inner mind
Impregnated and immersed
As it surpasses the compact human computer
Stored in the murky mass of messy cells
In our brilliant brain; active, agitated
We envision, exactly recall, digest by experience
So sensually sophisticated are we
That we evolve, develop, fathom
Rationalize into complicated patterns
The highest, greatest gift to humanity
Inspire infinite, incredible possibilities
A maturing prototype; compose, invent,
Unlike the finished product from a candy line production
Instead pray action, rebirth of who we are,
Carry our secret banner within our hearts
Aspire to god-like greatness
Almost touching the magnificent magic of the unreachable
Of who we were, who we are, and who we will become

≈ ≈ ≈

Be careful with spirited people – they are infectious

Some are so haughty and arrogant
That if they were an overblown balloon –
they would either blow up
or fly towards the moon.

Life Span

Am I a cackle, a bungler, a fool?
Have I learned nothing of life's painful school?
Is there no end to blabber and complain?
And if I err, can I please start again?

Did my dormant intellect come to affront
Or handicapped in the cesspool of life's pond
Oh, am I plain, a bit insane and vain
To dare tread in the mind of a reader again?

We; you and I, the composite, try to be true
Despite mistakes and failure we are here anew
With gusto act and live our creed
Anxious to climb the ladder of success indeed

Then somewhere in the herd a challenger obstructs
We fence, we fight, parry, bend and duck
To no avail; we meet our equal and admit
No more the chip on shoulder must be rid

We had and have our dances, love and some romances
Succeeded with our prowess, took some chances
But deep down finally our feet on earth
We've compromised and recognized our worth

Tempered by age certain wisdom is our treasure
Not by wealth and things, but within ourselves we measure
In gratitude for lifespan of observance of momentous events
Ready and willing to see if life and all this work makes sense

Now somewhat helpless we peruse our life about
Bit fearful that excess society might end in most explosive rout
Destructive, hedonistic, full of lust their choice
"Put on the brakes, society!" we shout with deafened voice

Despite success, grandeur and wealth
Somewhere, sometime nature soon deprives us of our health
Despite accomplishment and greatness we return to earth
Sadly that is and was our destiny from time of birth

Empty-Headed

The imbecile, the clown, and the hedonist
Particles of empty-headed romp around
Angels never did bless their head with a tender kiss
So audible, high pitch, the all-annoying sound

Some of these creatures so frivolous and silly
Ignore the danger, foolishness and pain
In frolic, rapacious laughs
Their empty lives sustain

And if a cute, cuddly lap dog
Our companionship must be
Our thoughts and action in a fog
Blind to the world to see

Thank god few nincompoops
The world does hope
And in some way gives recognition
They cannot cope (the dope)
Succumb in wasteland and derision

So steady, lucky YOU who think
So rational, with reason, motive and compulsion
Caution, yet full of hope and faith
Continue with future adventure unto special place
And in our imperfection find our human face

chapter three: world-wide adventures

See the World

How lucky , at any age, to jump on a plane or in a car to explore the world around us. Off to new vistas, near and far. Many of us unfortunately have not lived the excitement of visiting even the great corners of our own country. Wherever we live, there are great sights to see at our backdoor. From New England, New York and Washington, south to Florida, the Gulf of Mexico, stretching to the Midwest, onward to Los Angeles and San Francisco, Seattle or even Alaska and everything in between; the possibilities are endless.

We all know travel expands the mind, but it does much, much more. It pulls us from our value systems, our comfortable community in which we live, into new, different worlds. We learn tolerance and acceptance by traveling. Just the sounds and tempos, the accents, new foods and customs open our horizons; New Orleans beignets (powdered donuts), San Francisco sourdough bread or a Philly cheesesteak; the melting pots in the great cities, farm life in the Midwest, the tourist attractions.

When you travel, walking the streets, boulevards, parks, hopping on the local tram or bus, you cannot help but meet the friendliest, greatest people in the world. Despite their different dress, language and background, it is here were you interchange thoughts, customs, habit; learn to respect the individuality that differs in all of us.

Joy to Sunbathe

The tiny sand crystals so brightly on the beach do reflect
As ocean breezes each pebble kissed and touched
As if so pecked a panoramic shoreline vacation scene
So open, fresh and free; nature's blanket so inviting clean
A joy to sunbathe and reflect
Read to enjoy and feed my intellect
Sometimes I even got kissed

Too late, burned to a crisp

The Traveler

He,
so ignorant
will not find
proper shelter,
is lost, will wander.

His shadow follows him
even in the dead of night,
until
he
mysteriously
awakens.

31

Romance and Flirting On The Beach

Nearby a pristine ocean beach
Shapely model posed like juicy yellow-red peach
Sunbathed, slightly tanned, figure so admired
The tiny red two-piece bathing suit so readily inspired

Nearby, a blanket, a couple; hugs and kisses
Her halter strap shapely sexy on the misses
Ice boxes, low beach chairs, recliners
The beach a beehive of young adults with their minors

Young half-baked slim, appointed ladies
Risk their fate, display a tease to attract mate
Some chatty talk leads to romance
The young men eager take a chance

Far off a radio blasts hard rock
A group of youth dance, almost run amuck
Others smile, gyrate and wink in self-made style
Soon like honey bees staid languorously for a while

New friendships cement if chemistry just right
The beach adventure now a great delight
Romance accentuates most excitedly at twilight time
More physical, romance at its prime

Warm hugs, closeness, kisses, gentle massage
Lost pair of lovers now appear as a mirage
It's almost uncontrolled, found everywhere
This love bug testosterone with juice to spare

Call it infatuation or maybe love
Some heavenly word missile direct hit from above
We munch, we chew, cold drinks and beer
The sunbeam cook, we hit first gear

Great innocence and bliss pronounced on beach
With blanket, moonlight within reach

So free, abandon all inhibition
It's Mother Nature that blinds with indecision

The rest of life and strife and conflict still ahead
Most impossible challenges not yet met
Much promise in the coming year soon to arrive
While memories and fantasies of beach will long survive

Fork in Life's Road Traveled

All life is a contest
  The stakes are too high
    After all, isn't it your one and only
life?
      Years later:
      "If only I had..."
The fork in life's road traveled
  Your choice or several choices -
still yours!
    Precarious, risky
      Surefooted—never
        Chances—risk
You can fix things, but the people?
  "Forget it, forget them!"
    You cannot fix them
      Unless they have no soul
      Now at new crossroads
Wiser, more studied
  You have choices.
    "Will I make the right choice
      Next time?"
      Time so precious
Better to be decisive, than weasel
out
  Seems like it is not too late
    Yet it takes longer
      To recuperate after a false step
      Time now my nemesis
I am not clairvoyant
To act is to live
My choice! My time!

Waterfront, Gulf Coast, Florida

I am the remnant of another age
Traveled adventure of a sage
Magnified the beauty of our earth
Still have the painful scars to show my worth

To Beach and Freedom

Diet Snapple and ice tea
Still my thirst for simple fee
So absolute and resolute
Enhances laughter, healthy attitude

Perhaps a shot of bourbon would be better
Could imagine not following to the letter
It's not the hearty drink, but where I stand
Who I am with in this fair land

Or in ecstatic love mode so exact
Or in good humor, joke is cracked
Some critics in afternoon invite
Persuasive sharp debate that will excite

Relieved, now rested from such pressure
Can empty my mind and pocketbook at leisure
Conjure a flight to far off places
Where admirable disposition graces

Or rush to entertainment, always star struck
In repartee, debate and full of luck
In this utter freedom of the mind
A most delectable goddess I may find

Cavort at beach enraptured by the sight
Try to attract the maiden who seems absolutely right
Attend the brilliant lecture to enrich my brain
Or lecture others of the opportunities we gain

More cool drink on this so pleasant day
The tabloids and the news are more than I can say
Involved in conflict such as the periphery
Only deadly dreadful endings I can see

So better now discuss the mundane
The movies and the sports again
Latest gossip, behind scene and dessert
Problems in the neighborhood now on alert

School taxes raised again
Restrictive laws passed that are irrational and most insane
The latest concert musical or play
The foolishness in which we pass our day

And when the bell of old age reverberates in our ears
We simply do reflect on past and dears
Wonder what could have been and should have been
The boat we missed now leaves so lean

Adjusted to the new complacency and rest
And simply wish each other happiness and all the best
No chance for second chance with knowledge now obtained
To color world with new brush and new paint

༄ ༄ ༄

Holiday, lazy, conjure in bed
The whole day crazy with joy be fed.

Time Out

Jetsetters spend much time in the air
Wondering what's below, what's there
Oceans of wasteland yet to till
A curved earth we the people fill

Is it truly worth
Having so many of us here on earth
Or take this vision from the plane
And dutifully abstain?

Or sun lazily on the beach
Removing chains of the modern siege
Most precious time to think and rest
To revel and enjoy in your own nest

Those who contemplate and read
Fill in their life with study thoughtful seed

Vacation or retreats so necessary devised
Time for a person himself/herself be prized
Contemplate the meaning of self-worth
We know that time's so short on this holy earth

Piedmont 4th of July Parade,
CA 2013

Dig into the mind of any mature adult
And you will find and erratic genius
A sophisticated hidden voyager
ready to turn the world upside down

Only Morning

Fresh out of the crystal blue aquamarine fluid
Clean as a water rat
Scrambling for dry sand
What awaits?
Whom will I hug and kiss?
Whom will I miss?
My body shakes with joy
This blessed day is mine
To choose as I wish to do
Where is my beauty?
The bristling sun is scorching
Billions of brownish crystal sands
Each naked foot impresses
I search the beach, the blankets
My eyes now almost blinded by the sun
A heavenly, warm dire spirited day
There, under the beach umbrella
In the rainbow colored beach chair
There she is!
There is my towel
All so invigorating - natural "Hi, I am back!"
Blue sky, fresh air
Scenery, waves on water
And it is only morning!

≈ ≈ ≈

Travel widens your horizons
But when you return you will never be the same

There are many roads and directions,
the trick is to get off the couch and find the right one

Vacation

A mountain cottage by the lake
The little things I take
An extra key, flashlight and sun block
Pictionary, camera, Palm pilot, clock

A recording of My Love is Here to Stay
And one of American in Paris, cards to play
Silva's English Assassin novel, many sweets
Miscellaneous bundle of more treats

Grand vacation far away from home
The evergreens and pine trees, fields I roam
6000-foot mountain air to excite my mood
Away from communication in this interlude

Lofty, sumptuous meals, fish to be caught
Verbal expression and much intrinsic thought
Serenity with mountain lakes at my beck and call
An air of inner beauty for us all

Voyage
I hear the rumble of the engines outside
While here in my meditation center
Introspective, at turbulent peace
The energy of life sparks all around me
Inside my brain, potent and almost real

The creative mind is a trick
A creative, marvelous tool
Of a never-ending voyage
I can fill and empty my soul
Reach zenith of mountaintops

Consume all the elements of the heaven
All in moving, beauteous colors
Reach my own optimum, mental state
It is indeed an unbelievable voyage
Of heavenly proportion

Tropical Beach Vacation

Finally, foolishly escaped vacation
Transported to this lush green tropical isle
Near the equator - no gravity, humid air under a brilliant sun
All is laziness and lassitude
The myriad of snails cover pristine beaches
Beware of the undercurrent waves

The tropical scenery so serene is balanced
An ocean of space
Hues of blue with fauna of huge leaves
How did I ever isolate myself?
No desert, valley
Just the rich foliage of the ant-filled jungle

Steamy, tropical, decaying
With the rebirth of tropical onslaught
In my isolation there is time to contemplate
Suntan, let the warm water lap against my body
Sadly reflect – the world distant, real
Impotent, I watch the thousands of tiny crabs
Eke out their existence on the endless flotsam-laden beach

I want to be another Robinson Crusoe
Lazily, but guilt ridden, like Atlas,
I still carry the world on my shoulder
Here in Paradise, away – I call it vacation
Before they throw me back to the sharks of city conflict
Where I have to fight for my life

chapter four: sounds of flora and fauna

Mountain River, Sierra Mountains, CA

All Fades

The night is young
So is the morn
Until all fades
Into
Late afternoon
Sun sets
Golden glow
The end is near
Soon
A new beginning
Of my life
Can I live up to it?

Watching Birds

Never took time
To watch birds building nests
Too busy – school, work
One Spring I did
I left one world behind
Patiently – curiously
Each day into the woods
Watched as twigs, branches, added
To the nest by instinct and great labor
The female finally laid her eggs
I know the young ones hatched
Now I see birds everywhere

Nature

You, I, we are children of nature, so unique and natural, yet so distinctively different. We are all children of nature, endowed with natural rights, a life of liberty, equality, fraternity. How we use and abuse this power, control and manipulate, is another story. We are intellectually powerful, yet puny and often powerless against nature. Imagine having to live on nature's flora and fauna alone and battle against the elements. All emanates from nature; the miracle of your birth, the creativeness of your being and even the uncontrollable farewell, death, reverts us to the dust and gas whence we came from.

Yet, next to life, the greatest gift we have is to enjoy nature around us. Never underestimate what our planet has to offer. To respect nature. To love and fear nature which is truly US and everything around us and beneath us and above.

As a child I marveled; joyously running freely, catching the brown maybugs, smelling the leaves, the grass, even the dung from the meadow nearby where brown cows were grazing. Many of us tear ourselves away from the daily rat race to commingle with nature. We swim in the oceans, we ski the lofty mountains, we hike, we climb or simply meditate and stop the car at some scenic spot. Scared, we watch in awe as the distant tornado nears, or the river floodwaters swiftly cascade off the river banks, eroding all in its path. We run away from fires consuming thousands of precious acres, hope that droughts don't ruin our crops. We pray that the sick child's fever goes into remission. All are natural phenomena. Nature more than anything else cuts us down to size.

Please take advantage of nature's free gift and beauty. It may be your local park, your flower garden or the next scenic trip you have planned. Smell, feel, hear, see with intent and admiration nature's spectacles, too numerous to mention. And when you next itch to get out and move your body, think of finding nature to rejuvenate your mind. When you gaze at a waterfall, remember you are part of our world's natural family. When you dream, even nightmares are nature's way of reconstruction and purging memories. When you kiss the red, bursting cheek of a smiling baby – that's you colliding, interacting with nature.Just as you take care of yourself, so nature too should be preserved and cared for on a routine basis. Once you fall in love with nature it will be a heady affair, so watch out! I could write a whole set of encyclopedias just on nature, but my limited space leaves it up to you to discover nature, as you discover yourself.

Threshold of the Universe

With visions and fireworks
Pinnacle on Mount Loneliness
I experience the hues of the rainbow
Frothing, haunting formation of clouds
Cirrus, Nimbus - like angels, scaring demons in the sky
The radiance, the magnificence of life
Uncanny inspiration, all too short!

You and I stand on the threshold of this universe
Confined, deliberate - ready to dare or do
Planted firmly to explore our vision
Open eyed, with little trepidation
Gift of life in all its brilliance
Like Moses holding the tablet of the
Ten Commandments

Downward - exhorting his people
To abandon the Golden Calf
So you too - here -
Retreat from the steep mountain
Inspired/halo - visionary
Truth - in awe of The Creator
The Unifier of the Universe
Queen/King of nature's power

Admiring, thankful, humble
In this, our place, the infinite universe
The spirit is within you - me!
Yet, we are but on the threshold!
Go, take another first step!

I love to cuddle with my dog or with my cat
In truth I prefer people
One at a time,
But dogs and cats don't talk back.

Sunlight

In small shapes I see
Hues reflected against the clouds
Cool pinks, shades, variations
Each so distinct, so pristine
Lemon, purple, orange
Translucent
Tomato, pear, apple
Strawberry succulent
Yet it's the bright sun's glow
Slowly diminishing at the horizon.
Glistening, retreating
Often penetrating the fluttering leaves
Attached are tiny bugs, invaders migrants
Leave dancing mottled shadows
The symmetry of clouds and light, all green
Red, purple, moving in the wind
With even moving white clouds reflecting now seen
Picture postcard perfect
In scenic awe, with my own eyes
My own world
As the last glimpse of light dives on the horizon

Mosquito

Mosquito with its thin legs doesn't mind
Pierces my sleep and sucks me blind
Invades my bed like it is king
Too late, blood sucker, I feel the itch and sting
From under the blanket buzz around my head
I aim the fly swatter
Now at least one is bloody dead

Flowers

Wonders to share;
Fragrant pink roses,
Red tulips, dalias, mums

The red, yellow blossoms
Bouquet, rich colored blooms
Visual blessings from nature's bosom

With perfume fragrance into the house
The world outside now so within
But lifeline cut, the stems suck water

The flowers, distant from their warmth soon fade
Will wilt and spoil, sadly to be discarded
But you and I outlast those flowers

Our memories latched to their sunshine state
So lucky, I'll bring you more flowers soon!
Another rainbow cascade

Fleeting, relish in their gratifying beauty
Before the exhilaration pales
In the recess of our memory
Ours to behold for our lifetime

≈ ≈ ≈

Tsunami shakes the ebb and flow
Into a wall of water, ripple to a blow
Soon flooded town and ocean beach
Can't stop nature's strength or reach

Near Lake Tahoe, Sierras, CA

California Fall

So lucky now, a balance act
      There is the constant, warm
California sun, happily diffused
      Everywhere, the golden brown hills and autumn trees
          Meadows, crops, gardens with lilies
             and poppies
And other white interlopers
      Over the last blanket of color

It is a rich, somber, yet fruitful season
If only my life resembled this splendid comforter
My heart drums its own rhythm
      My mind blown like fireworks in flux
          Celebrate nature's potpourri of gyrating colors
          all this

Before the onslaught of winter
∾ ∾ ∾

Amazing how a little wooden splinter
Or a mosquito bite can bring us down to earth,
Cloud our miserable minds
Poor me! Cure me!

The Banks Of A Bubbling Brook

Come, come and see
Coyote, and jackrabbit, black bird
Do come with me as joyful hand in hand we wander
Let's hike the gorgeous rocky brown mountain roads
Sit on gray rock on the banks of the bubbling brook
The music of the rippling, roaring rush
The croaking of the toads
The light, refreshing breeze against my cheeks
And you so beautifully beside me,
So sensual, tender warm tender hands, embrace
Like in a storybook
Or long-forgotten dream
Soon overcome our bashfulness
Soft kisses, smell of perfume, some fondling, now a charm
Put blanket on a soft, moist green
So quickly our loving time in the vast meadow
Mesh with the chirping bird, the rustle of the grass
The vast unending sky a silent happy witness
Evaporating the anxious in heart's romantic cure
Of our love so innocent and pure
Oblivious of dancing sunbeam, rustling branches
So privileged, private our space, under natures colorful canvass
To care, to share, to love albeit but a minute fraction of our life

Within The Forest

The rare silhouette moves on
Tramps   on   the mushy
          damp decayed   leaves
             within the dense dark forest
Charm its rare visitors
Majestic, steadfast trees intimidate
Lifeless, curious almost absorbed
Looking down at this tiny figure; me
Yet in a parental, protective manner

I feel sucked in by the brown leafy forest
Slithering within the moist decayed vegetation
I feel like a midget amongst giants
          Yet safe, serene, peaceful
             all is fascinating.

I move in forward slow motion
Branches' leaves; a yellowish huge slug, spider webs
Maybe a newt or two stumble to safety under the leaves
Amazing! All this will be here long after me
To share such a holy, heavenly spirit
The pungent smell of dying needles
          what a precious present
            our Gods give us here!

All I have to do is search it out to be
And here I am in this heavenly arena of flora, fauna
The tops of the tall trees touching blue sky
        And I, a lucky two-legged voyager
         I once again discover and wonder

~ ~ ~

The sunny bright day cheers the heart
But as we age, more sedentary
We respect nature more
Still, an apple a day is still in the cards
Little things in life are the pearls of the day

47

We Monkeys

Some monkeys hang so upside-down by tail
And fly from branch to branch as if to hail
Free-spirited, enthusiastic with their kind
Oblivious to other monkey tribes so blind…

Now naturalists come to study those apes
Take their pictures and get their grunts on tapes
An irritant, a scare, a cage
Remaining monkeys fearful, enraged

When their habitat is interrupted
With source of food now corrupted
In our reflection we see the monkey's last dance
Stripped of old freedoms - never had a chance

What right to interrupt their love life
Or if the brute now has third wife
No more to forage for his food
And spend his life exhibit in the nude

View from the Plane

Like a master bird, wings spread afar
The fissures of topography far below like arteries
Scan mountaintops and plains
Peruse life and world in momentary fleeting sights

The eagle eye views our plateau of achievement
The arid dry waste endless, forbidden below
Unlike the rich chapters in our lives
Recalled, scanned, not forgotten

Below a vast expanse of country
Like the recall of treasured memories
The roads and highways; our travels
Recounting hectic and eventful lives

And the mother of great ravines
That slowly move, vast expanses
Where, when we land, let it all out
Always recall the beautiful eyes and faces

There are vast shores of lakes
Like the limitations in our lives
From mountain peaks to oceans below
Showing our illuminations

Dances, graduations, travels
Merry raucous parties
Lovemaking at its best
As we live and learn, visually wonder in amazement

High above are heavy gray cumulous clouds
What a panorama, what a landscape!
What magnificent vistas we cover in our
Wonderful, amazing, mostly happy lives

Our chores, our duties and obligations;
Child raising, scaling the job ladder like ants on the earthy crust
Too busy to appreciate nature's miracles and gifts
Yet doggedly thankful to challenge the next day

Yes, we are temporary giants on earth
Lifetime to educate and acquire a ton of goods
As we thrive for inner happiness
And leave all that junk behind when the time comes
Acknowledging it was quite a trip

chapter five: ghosts and apparitions

"Dreams"

Merriam Webster says dreams are the thoughts, images or emotions during sleep. I am not going to compete against Doctor Freud, yet much poetry is a dreamlike state, a cross between the real and unreal. After all, our sub-conscious mind is in constant play. Events from childhood, usually fear complexes, lay unresolved. For example, I may find myself in some resort or scout camp in the country, part of a group. The group is ready to return home, but I frantically scamper to get my suitcase and goods, and miss the bus and feel stranded.

Today I am a widower, have a two-story house with all the goodies, packed library, an ultra-modern kitchen, fenced spacious yard, very secure indeed. Yet when I dream there is a fear complex, an unresolved feeling of abandonment, even by my wife who appears from time to time, after a solid forty-four year marriage. Ten or eleven years after my Mother died, I suddenly communicated in a dream with her until I woke up. All these dreams are unfilled, incomplete. When I am physically lost in my dreams I used my creative ingenuity to find ways to escape. If I am lost in the country, I will find a highway and hitchhike toward a safe haven. Occasionally I will challenge and fight, but more often I will escape with a survival instinct. Sometimes I am not caught, but escape on my own.

Your Dream

Not as a dream
A wink, all disappears
Like a trained magician
His black suit
But the rabbit is squeezed behind mirrors
Its heart is beating
The magic of returning
And so your dream
Will reappear
Not as a dream

Night Noise

4:30 A.M., now suddenly awake
A noise, a bang somewhere a suspiscious break
As if a witch or ghost
Is here to entertain, to raise me a toast
Half drowsed, the other half alert
Did knocking sparrow enter as a bird?
Alas, it is but an unlocked window gone awry
And not a dangerous
Martian spy!
Now so awake, I can't go to sleep

Already counted eight hundred sheep

Ghost

Come my ghost, play with me!
It was but last night that your lips met mine
So luscious, warm, soft, begging
Chased you before you vanished
Bereft, worried, concerned
What devil's play concocted?
Disappearance — you lurk near by
I know it — feel it
Come, ghost, bring back that idle youth
The dreamer, whose eyes melt
With visions of tomorrow
Inducted in the teenage art of love
So clumsy, yet driven by desire
I sense you still — behind the wall
In lurking shadow, close, so close
But then I remember the accident
Can happen, did happen
You left me — bereft me
All is forgiven
But only after I awake fully
As guilt and innocence and sweat
Bring wonder all so real
That I can almost touch you, ghost now

≈ ≈ ≈

He cried for help
Vocal cords cut
No one could hear him

The Moon

The moon so glowing, shows so full
Its craters, shadows and magnetic pull
Its valleys, mountains, so well designed
What a magic distant spot I hope to find!

Ghosts of My Ancestors

Join my last ride –
The ghosts of my Jewish ancestors
Looking over my shoulder –
Moses, Abraham, Isaac, Jacob
Potent, prophetic posterity
They breathe the air of truth
Family, charity, respect, gratitude
Infused hope of mankind

If I may digress – Carved in my brain
My forefathers engraved
The values, dignity of each
In resurgence of moderation, tolerance, respect
Belief in self, act out in deed and action
Tower above – resist the heathen temptations
Of blind seduction or gross conquest of flesh
Rue torture and submission

Feed my ego in our climb to the top
Resist abundance and the acquisition of goods
Instead, learn; knowledge, prayer
Exude love and compassion, forgiveness
The Torah our cornerstone of humanity
That ancient wisdom feeds our human soul
Empties treasures from the recesses of our mind
And separates us from all others

I am that aged soul, a continuum of generations
Experienced much in this tumultuous world
Laugh often – proud and grateful
Yet I carry the scars of loss and failure
Nothing is forever – except infinity
But it's a hell of a ride
Throughout, the chain of love;
Love for family, friends, dear ones
Especially for myself

Ethics, morals, so deeply ingrained from childhood
It is a proud standard I carry on this great journey
And I believe the next few chapters of my life
Will be rich, exciting, full of love for mankind
An era of deep sharing and giving

Why not join me now in another chapter
In our charismatic world
On our final ride?

His Shadow Follows Him

He
So ignorant
Will not find
Proper
Shelter
Lost
Wander
His shadow
Follows him
No escape
Even in the
Dead
Of
Night

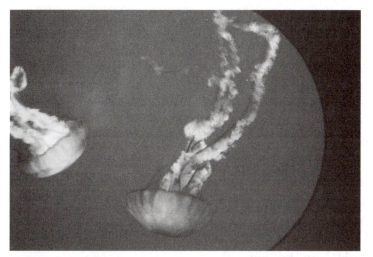

Jellyfish Exhibit,
Monterey Aquarium,
CA

To Relax

To relax
Completely
I put on brakes
Wipe out all meaning

Let space be my vehicle
Transparent, eyes closed awhile
Now eyes newly open to
serenity
Slow breathing
An inner world apart

A smile – in solitude I touch the
world

Visions, apparitions, dreams
In space, weightless

The world touches me most gently
Keenly alert

Infinite wonderful possibilities

Was the Trip Worth it?

Inebriated, soused
Incoherent state
Not a drop of alcohol
Nor mind-bending drugs
Just dizzy from day's dance
As dictated
Tempos, frequent movement
With ease at first
Soon the dance rhythmic
Next athletic and
Finally followed beat in free form
Whole body, frenetic, twisting
Until so absorbed
Pirated, blown out of water
Almost amnesia
Into an unacceptable state
Yet wild abandonment
One of checks, bribes, confusion –
Recover; sleep it out
Was this trip really worth it?

The Skeleton Remains

Grotesque
Like an ugly fish
The beast
that
Gnarls and snarls
Inedible
The dish
An eerie plate of
gruesome fare
The skeleton remains
Scary, eerie

࿎ ࿎ ࿎

It's OK to dream standing up...

At Peace

The magic wand of eye fatigue
    Colored spectrum into gray

Blurred focus
    Brings all I value into oblivion

The eyelids say, "Close"
    The body says, "Recline"

Breathe slowly
    Anxiety melts

And the massive Queen of Slumber
    Rules for awhile

So, please don't press me for help
    For decisions now

For commitments or deeds
    Nature's way to repair, replace

You know my fatigue will wear out
    Reality again will stare at me with both barrels

Should I shoot first?
    Or return to Nirvana?

Or remain in this post-hypnotic state

At peace?

Momentary Confusion

Before awakening within
To life unfettered, in a trance
The dormant mind so full of visions

In glorious, fresh, morning bed
Eyes still closed, arms eagle spread
Slowly as the chick hacks its way to freedom

Relaxing aura
Heart and chest react
Repose in stillness

Experience again
Half dream of beauty
Blinded, ecstatic

Where sun and sky and ocean meet
From shadow molded vision
Fade into unending horizon

Timeless flashes of past
Faces so real, almost can touch
In rapture, spirit talks

Immobile, frozen, past fear, confront
My subconscious fabricates
Can smell the sorcerer approaching

Only seconds more – heavy sweat
Awaken as if colliding with my tomb
Still frozen in cement – must extricate

So agitated, I awake
Angel and devil, precarious on the cliff of paradise
Can it be real – what was, what is?
Momentary confusion
Scary

A Quilt of all Occasions

A quilt of feelings
Emotions knit into the
Fabric of my being

Truth, beauty, love, honor
The colors are my cornerstone
Yet ocean waves whittle away
My morality, all so embedded in the cloth
        New aspects of truth

What is so truly right and wrong
The many shades now in-between
Vast layers of hidden beauty rediscovered
Passions of love
        stimulated by six senses

So I cover myself, dazzled with the
Old patterns, my beautiful quilt
My truth, my value of beauty
        My emotional involvement of love

Trying to retain some sense of balance
Lest my honor be shattered
Bombarded by the day's deeds
I recline, pull the quilt over my body
        Cover and soon fall into a trance

A kaleidoscope of my life
While it lasts, so many values, so many pieces
The bond of love and chemistry foremost
        A quilt of all occasions

*Benny Bufano
mosaic mural,
Oakland, CA*

chapter six: more than words

These New Poets

These new poets
Spin words like strands of silver
On golden tongues
Glue phrases or chisel them
Into our minds
Unload their feelings on us
Into riveting sentences
From mind and body, ego filled

Raise beauty up to heaven
Then drop their victim
Crashing into eternal hell
Preserved and pinned
Called grace
Take flower, fauna
Illuminated, hewn like roman statues
Nature's beauty so blind
That once in love with beauty
It is robbed as seasons change

These new uplifting poets
Authorize the art of the erotic
Cut from gauzy, gaudy cloth
Severing of body parts
Declaim the cruelties of war

Yet I love their rhythm
The sensitivity
Their wake-up call
Forbidding warnings
Colorful world pictures

Stern prophesies of tomorrow
And life situations of today
Can we hold onto our senses, our health?
We, your egotistical poets, irritants within us

Bastards of language, full of paranoia
Where will you send me next?
What great revelation?
The crucifixion was two millennia ago
Wasn't that enough?

Poetic License

Poetic license stretches surreal
Even to sundown's horizon
Dawning revelations
A touch of infinity; careful phrasing
Do not overstep!
A heap of trouble once in print
No place to hide once exposed
The power of the word
Has decimated many a giant.
Careful – lest you wish to ignite humanity
Foster change, revolution
Catapult the world doldrums
And want a statue
Named after you

Does every story have to have an abundance of words?
Aren't meaning and feeling enough?

Gibberish

Gibberish; the babe's peculiar gargles must have some meaning such as "I want milk!", or "I want it now!" for free, immediate consolation.

So too, in later development as an adult, much language is still gibberish, shallow, almost meaningless. When many citizens talk gibberish the country is fraught with danger, their voting sensibility is shallow and uneducated, ill-informed, about to lose the free and open society they live in.

Even the Orangutan has some limited vocabulary, they tell me...

It's our parents, our public school system and mostly the media that brings us down to a low common denominator. Let's degenerate to the level of a twelve year-old in our vocabulary, let's avoid thinking, and just listen to the latest music, no matter how loud or disjointed, and talk gibberish.

It is not only speech, but also thoughts expressed; iPhones, Droids, iPods, iPads, Tablets still need us to control them and provide content. Only education, purpose and a greater zeal for combined knowledge will result. We absolutely need to become a more articulate, educated people with purpose and conviction again to communicate better.

Still, it is not only in the gibberish talk, but also in the act of doing by which our nation and civilization will be measured. Remember some of this gibberish and misunderstandings have turned into bloody wars.

Writing is a self-fulfilling prophecy
It comes from within your head
Put there and excavated
For a better day

If you say too much it can be dangerous
If you write and expose yourself, it may be deadly
And may end up on your tombstone

Prolific Writing

Paper is cheap
Yet writing on it prolific
Words into life
Colored pictures
Excite the senses
Emulate the world
Feed the imagination
Nature, mankind under the microscope
Eyed this very moment
Transcribed into a hundred languages
From print focused to brain
Or saved on some computer chip
Past – future and the now displayed
Brain translated – osmosis – sponged
Stir feelings and emotion
Descriptive, good writing a rarity, an art
Yet we sense, we feel, we visualize
Philosophies, dreams and ideas
Like sparks, some transcend
Transcribed into a living start
If you run out of paper
Lost your computer chip
You have denied the world much

Read in Silence

The glowing neon lamp diffusing light
makes waning day bright
I read these special notes
in silence overcome
With salty tears
Mine

If Words

If words
Strong
Accusative
Were only in Sanskrit
Or in Hebrew, Arabic
Or Latin or Chinese
In ignorance unknowing
I would not object
But in my language
A false accusation
Destructive innuendo
Addressed to me
Is like a pesky flu – aggravating
I feel it – must combat it
Inexcusable, unsettling
Best to preserve the truth
Undeserving – time consuming
I will survive this pestilence
No need to redefine
Just tell, write
the Truth

Your Turn Will Come

I never finished reading
that book
sort of dropped out of it
sitting lonely now on the
shelf
replaced, like she
by another
don't judge
your turn will come

Words Touched

So much to share and tell!
Some ideas fabricated – others I know well
But you, dear reader,
Can turn the page any time!
Toss my book, or lap up every line
Or erase me out of your mind
And go routinely as you are – missed out and blind
You, dear reader, are creative; do not need kings
You can combat vegetation and the nothingness of things!

To read is to enrich
Words - meaning - retention
Have their coy intention
So many tongues, so many phrases
In truth, most go to blazes
The gift to share from mind to find
What greater pleasure can you find?

Paint the World

They are all poets
We are all poets
Portray the extreme
Make the flowers smell
Paint the world with rainbow colors
Extremes of orange, grass green

Yet flag the stormy clouds
With warning greys
Backed by pure black
The night heaven hides
White earthly creatures maneuver
Fight, jostle, dig and procreate

Until the weary morning hours
and nature rings the bell of exhaustion

Read

Read! Yes relax, tear yourself away. Read!
Fiction incarnated
Folly of family disillusion, incest, murder
Famous and infamous
Read lots!
Your inspiration will grow
Your mind will bulge, blow up like a balloon
The secret suitor; murderer
Connection to the heist, intrigue
Fed by words into fantastic scenes
Stuffed with curiosity
Stimulate and marvel at the expansive realm of nature
All painted word pictures
Ideas, visualization, metaphors
Novels, biographies, science all at your fingertips
Solve mysteries, create new ones
The mind, imaginary and real
Spooky, scary, scandalous chameleon of character
Yours to challenge, to traverse
These endless word pictures of possibilities
All yours with open mind and eyes to treasure!
Or the wisdom of Aristotle, Homer, Einstein
Read about economic disaster,
Spring planting, soccer
Or even the gruesome, torturous Holocaust
Read about starvation, global warming
Astronauts in space, Hollywood legends
Babies growing up, love and platitudes and beliefs
A basketful of mish-mash
Once sorted out, oh what pearls!
What treasures! Even forensic laboratories
Caught but not convicted yet
Ramification - implication - scandal
And you don't even have to say Obama

Words

Words – some like feathers
Some like lava stones
Descend with dusty, deadly force
Letters pronounced, leave their mark
Announce revolution – call for change
No more the status quo
The haves and have-nots locking horns
Continents on fire; armies ready
Folly and insanity
Leveling populations

Zealots with religious blindness –
We are not yet ready to escape to other planets!
When will the insatiable insanity stop?
Avarice, jealousy, ego and hate
Shrouded in the name of preservation
This need to protect, secure, control
Are the gods in heaven betting on the outcome?
Do we, mortals at the zenith of our history
Have to be imbeciles and start over?

Stop us! Where are you, Judge – Empire?
The flood of tears and war
The menace of self-destruction
Is near –
Words into peace offerings
Melt our hearts and pray for reason
Has no one ever heard of World Peace?
Heaven help us!

How are my words meaningful?
Where do words fall? Have you witnessed the corpses?
Musty now, who picks them up?
What shall I do with them?

WORDS LIVE ON

My poem is like a morsel, a crumb
Jettisoned somewhere on the Internet
Millions can read them - free
Tearful tales of love entwined

As the blinding fog disappears under the sun's beams
So, too, my bond at a fragile juncture dissipates
Observed by an accidental Internet visitor
Who gorges on my heavenly words
As if having digested delicious pasta
Reiterates: "I will always love you!"

That resonant voice of anonymous encouragement
Of invitation, transcending
Somewhere on that magical Internet
Right here, visible
In blinded spirit of idyllic hope
The whisper for forgiveness

Despite imminent parting
As it says: "I will always love you!"
The words echo, yet the chemistry has worn off
No more the eternal, haunting spirit
Of ghosts in a huddle, protecting
All is on the solid footing of now
That marvelous feeling is dissipating
Fingers intertwined like Adam and Eve
In their virginal garden fraught with temptation

Words turned to mesmerizing visions
Of good, of beauty - before the fall
All so descriptive, solid and prophetic
Until the dismal foreboding phrase: "We must part!"
We scatter as our love withers, decays, dies
As each of us ventures into new directions
Yet from the distance a faint echo

"I will always love you"

Duplicated, etched deeply in the computer's heart
But words live on
Inscribed, on someone's computer
Haunting, eerie
Shot, transported by search engines
To confused and hypnotized readers
Who'd think today is here forever?
Tomorrow always exists
Careful, curtain's down
Finality is around the corner
But the words live on
And somewhere even our ancestor's soul
Hovers above

Often I just don't know
But can't admit it

Help, Help, I'm Drowning

Evening – recline
First one shoe off
Then sticky stocking
As these virgin words
Flow faster from me
As I watch the second shoe drop
Disrobe completely
Each time I write another line
Now naked in my birthday suit
Plead innocent
The avalanche of words won't stop
Help!
Help!
I am drowning in words!
Call in the deeds to help
An irresistible stream of more words
Lifeguard not here, you say
Off duty tonight!
Help!
I'm drowning!

chapter seven: provoking the grey matter

Meditative Thought

No matter how poor or rich
Tonight before eyes close
Escape your niche
Meditate. Reflect. Pray with dignity.
Inquire, with self-intospection, in a corner of your room
Where peace, compassion now do loom
Silently, eyes opened or close
Relax, breathe heavy out of mouth and nose
In contrast to the litany of a hectic day
The power of the spirit now holds sway
gone, nothing to lose
Material wealth replaced not choose
Prophetic inspiration of your "id"
This moment is yours to make your bid
Dream-like, find salve for your pains
Contracted angels upheld in chains
Unfurled, nourished, sustained, new venues now unfurled
Confusing aspects of our more macabre world
Tired, utter fatigue, I now retreat, almost asleep
Timeout, at ease, a covenant to keep
Which virtue won?
Which temptations now undone?
I close my eyes, I yawn
Weaker, tired, like a pawn
One aspect: sleep ignore
The other: face the spirit to the core
Were food, the clothes soon to disappear
Stripped of my outer garments
I am what I am
Still here

Do Not Ask

Do not ask I'm disillusioned
For the task,
So do not ask
My thoughts, desires elsewhere
Simply I reject,
Don't care at this time
So do not ask
But if you do respect
My thoughts and intellect
Make room and let me read
But do not ask
Let me consume with deed of nothing
As I am nothing now
Absorbed in my own orbit
But do not ask
You know we all get that way sometimes

On a Precipice

On a precipice
The edge
Abyss below
Cautious walk on path
Conscious of life and death
Separated by one last breath
So we make our way
Knowing full well
That what comes next
It is the uncertainty
Feelings, dreamlike
Not blind to ourselves

～ ～ ～

If you dig too deep into the soul
The dangerous, honest truth will soon come out
And more

I REFLECT

Reflect on those masterful experiences
A dash of the landscape of life
Kaleidoscope of happening
With hoe and rake and tractor
Final test; infatuation, love
Jeff, Judy; gems, shine, grow, learn
Lecture in front of thousands
Veteran, teacher, real estate broker, lover
Elevated, respected.
Writer.
Theater aficionado, books, poetry
The gentle faces eye to eye
I do not dare look into the mirror
Let the jet zoom, flit by
It's a glorious, rough, real
Laughing life, left in tears
Despite setbacks, grateful, thankful
Wisdom, wealth, cremated
Without me, I reflect again
Silent - quiet - gone - gone!

Philosophic Love and Life

Thomas Aquinas, Hegel, Kant
Nietzsche, intellectually profound
In our thoughts most heavenly bound
Mired - we are in need
Of new philosophy indeed

Pragmatic, spiritual to suit this life and time
Rational, inspired, most uplifting and poetically rhyme
Away from conflict and from war
Instead we'll search for peace and more

Yet in revolution do we thrive
Examine change with sharpest knife
Have riddles answered
A surviving dancer

Balance between life and death
First to experience knowledge
Life – living – now our college
Caution and wisdom, qualities to boot
Success and optimism, mental food
Balanced between world's rights and wrongs
In love, right here we do belong

Choose limb and life, want to be understood
Proud praise and hail all that is
All races in our brotherhood
Hammer wisdom into true belief
With tolerance that all receive

Think – adjust to need of change
More sensible, new order, all arrange
Awaken mankind to new time and place
Strive for the just, humility and grace

Sparkle – new hope and humor high
Respect all living, none deny
In awe, in image of the maker be
Grow, prosper like a full-spread tree

Grow in life's compost rich and strong
Deep love of mankind, ours to belong
Actively embrace the beauty that's within
Consider all mankind
Your precious loving kin

Each moment, hours strive to heal
Rejuvenate, self-satisfaction be your wheel
And in a thousand ways more love again
Yes, love yourself in sumptuous and delirious vein
Your being, and now your anchor, will sustain

Some of the best ideas and thoughts
Come out of the most unexpected moments
Treasure, remember them
Write them down
And for the rest of your life
Figure out their meaning

Far ahead

Jumpstart for some, race far ahead
Adrenaline, anxious spells without regret
First to hit the ball perfectly correct
Open left field and gain respect
Study and "practice, more practice" have their reward
Bat, pitcher, catch, know when to play your card
Euphoric when your friends do cheer
Respected, cheered on, you are dear
But after new and awful training, you're a bust
Know life is a competition, full of lust
Sometimes you have to change the sport
Leave venue, fly now to another port
Constantly your ego, body feed
Satisfied, anxious to challenge and compete
To win and overtake the goal
Does have its price, you pay the toll

Demonstration, Ferry Building, San Francisco, CA

A PRAYER

It's OK, in busy times or sorrow or joyous
To take time out to meditate
Yes, pray – so I pray
For forgiveness, good tidings
Heal me, help me, oh, most powerful
Mystic spirit, father, mother

Yes, yes, I feel wounded. I have sinned
I have wronged, lied, deceived, and cheated
Still, I want to be healed
I want to cleanse my soul

I am but human flesh under the canopy of heavens
So I pray to you for guidance
For forgiveness, for sunshine and bountiful rain
For great crops and magnificent inventions to aid mankind
I pray to you to safeguard my flesh, my family, my community
I pray to you to give guidance to our leaders
Let them compromise and sustain peace and tranquility

I pray that anger and hate dissipate into kindness,
Love and understanding
I know my time on earth is limited
So let goodness and benevolence exude from me
Oh mighty spirit, father, mother, universe
Make me whole again, a son or daughter worthy of you
And cleanse my body from evil thoughts and deeds
So that I may be a true servant to mankind

So help me heaven

≈ ≈ ≈

I vacillate from one idea to
Nothing

Tiger in Waiting

I feel like a precursor predator stalking
A tiger laying waiting for the wildebeest
Instinct and self-preservation
For she carries the riddle
The perfect seed of mankind
The mutation.
Food, fangs and all
Awaiting the punch line.
With her heroic strength and agility
Brilliant repartee, master,
Encyclopedic memory.
I pant.
Manly, full of testosterone
Handsome, athletic,
The second seed.
Ingrained, determined and prolific
I pounce on the bandwagon
Hurrah for adulation, hero worship,
For abstract love, for fornication
Shatter the bands into total freedom
Let me be myself
Like the tiger in waiting.

Anonymous Gift

The gift anonymous
Another anonymous
Composer anonymous
Witness anonymous
Painter anonymous
Why don't we know?
Or do we always have to
Place a plaque
Where earth was transformed
Into rich forest
Abounding with nature
The fish, the lizard
Then finally the monkey
Who took the inanimate?
Breathed life?
The genius of intelligence, survival
Who – what – created the races of mankind
In all its shapes and forms, religions and beliefs?

Times change, people change
The mystery unanswered
Then there is me –
Anonymous gift
I want you to know
Is my donation meaningful?
It is MY gift! My life!
So insignificant compared to heaven's clouds
So what? It is a gift – my token – anonymous
Short time to be remembered
A proud, braggadocio
Still my gift

Anonymous – exposed to the world
Avaricious in every way – anonymous
Yet the colossus, the mystic, an apparition
Created the monster of evil
And the angel of love and goodness

Most ideas fizz like Coke,
so act, before the effervescence dissipates

Sternness

It's more
Exciting
To sit down
Comfortably
Contemplate
Sights and
Ideas
Not to be
Shocked
Or interrupted
By the
Sternness
Of the
Seat

Pontificate

I sometimes pontificate ·
Proud of my accomplishments
In how I rate
Ego inflate
In great exuberance still
If I don't do it, then who will?

Of course, it's the ways I do it that really count!
To what degree and what amount?
A trifle here, a holler there
To which extent I boast my fare
And my glorification depends
How breakfast, and my outlook blends
The rejection could be a heavy blow

Agony of Not Knowing

Sometimes the agony of
not knowing
Supersedes the agony
of knowing

Is it cancer or not?
Heart attack or an arterial block?
Will it leave and then come back
or somewhere else attack?

Is it a boy or a girl?
Healthy child like a precious pearl?
Do you love me
or just pretend and see?

I'm competitive - can I win
or lose and lightly take it on the chin?
Did I pass the test
Or fail and fake the rest?

Do I really love her, enamored by her magic wand?
Brainy, quick, dubious decision, not so hard
This I know - I still can dream
Vital, lively get my share of cream
Avoid conflict, strive
Grateful, can discern, so very much alive

Quit while I'm ahead
Or competition may strike me dead

≈ ≈ ≈

After you add it all up,
Is there more wisdom in the restful morning
Or the adventurous night?

chapter eight: it's not all luck

I kando, and you can do too!

You, I, all of us, can do much to feel better. I am a good person, I punch holes in my daily life. Yes, I am imperfect, but I am that moving, growing, creative creature called human, just like you.

A hidden dream – I can do it! From my sub-conscience, a secret spirit would pop up at the oddest times. "You can do it!"

I want to share with the world thoughts of the most intimate nature, thoughts of deep conviction, of love, of religious belief, of deep faith in the survival of mankind, so short lived.

I am ready to go to sleep. Two thirty A.M. – yes, that's way beyond most people's bedtime. Yet, like a zombie, a ghost in my pajamas, I tread toward the study. There is something driven in me. I am uncontrollably excited. It is as if some religious demand and occasion is pushing me into action. Any inaction, relax, sleep, would only be fraught with tomorrow morning's guilt.

"Yes, you can!" is the silent, overpowering motto, dizzily spinning within my brain. Is it that my life is ending soon, despite no frightening disease? Is it that strong ego that we all harbor – like the thief on a prowl, the addict ready for his fix, the runner ready to compete within himself?

"Yes I can!"

I am going to write the "Kan feel good" essay – for me, for you, for my ego, for respect of my children who long ago have written off my intellect and write it off as an old geezer in a frenetic stage asking for recognition.

Actually, it is all of these.

All this is a wonderful synthesis of why life is beautiful. Why things will stay good for me and even better in the future. All based on the foundations of a dash of hope. We have choices. Why not be happier, more fulfilled, laugh more and keep that "feel good" deep inside, so rich, spiritual and strengthening.

Can you feel better? "Of course!"
Can you do better? "Of course!"
Can you succeed? "Naturally!"

So in the coming pages, common sense, no empirical study, I will share and hopefully you too will share with me. "Yes I can!"

80

My Wish For You

Dare — take time to peruse and read
Share my hopes, my wishes — dreams

Identify or disagree with love's struggles
Radiant smiles — but read, reflect, imbibe

You, the reader — blessed
As you escape into the imaginary world
Of senses

A world of feeling and emotions
The baby's cry, the lover's exultation

The philosopher, the cursing soldier
The benevolent patrician
All make appearances

You link with my thoughts
Link with my enormous dreams

You give me the greatest gift
As you let me tease your brain

With truths and contradictions
Muse your mind with my ramblings

Hear my echo saying:
Thank you!

Thank you
For the time we mingled

I'm So Lucky

I'm so lucky
To be here
Alive!

Cherish this moment
Sipping this drink
Gulping a bite
Eyes eat up action
Whispering noises
Breeze against my cheek
Rejoice
Smile as taste buds are jubilant
Anxious to share

This very moment
With you
With friend, twice celebrated
My mind stuffed
Filled with pleasure
Appetite just right
Tease for more
This is the innocent void
Simple thought
Heartbeat of freedom
Of now –
Is what I see, I feel, no pain?
Oh yes, life's price
No thought of whining
At peace – few complaints

Flashes of love, the sensual
To gently touch you, stroke you
Hold you – ravish you
Here – now
With curtain drawn
Yes, facial muscles completely relaxed
In silence – I am so lucky
So rapt – I want all to stand still
In a picture frame of happiness
Inhale the spirit of this moment
Euphoric, physical, self-satisfied

Until someone suddenly interrupts:
Angrily, quizzically
 "Did you know?
There is a bloody war out there?"

Never Too Late

Never too late to tolerate
With kindness put up with
Those you hate
Dull your thought
Blind hate, rational hate
Hate — hate!
Your feelings overwrought
Each of us destined to our fate
No choice
Can we learn to live and tolerate
Or leave this world with this gruesome feeling?
Can we fend off the feelings of the enemy's hate,
Before it is too late
Lest you, I, too become infected, so destructive
Like our adversary
Like a cancer, hate eats goods of humanity
I try to forgive, I try to forget.
Yet, the disease is infested, tirelessly reoccurs.

Live life,
Partake with friends
Pursue your dream of satisfaction
Good food, lots of love and action
Squash the hatred, push it on the garbage heap
Celebrate!

It's not easy. But then what is?
A great challenge!

≿ ≿ ≿

It's OK to pick other people's brains
and tailor the best ideas for yourself
And receive well-earned compliments for your efforts

Simple

Our small race has much to offer
But often do not know how to dish it out
Some stay paupers
many become rich
and most of us are busy
work, love, children
and have no time for war

Pass the Test

It is OK to recharge your batteries for a new start
And place new goals before your cart
Earn, you learn, for vistas new now await
It's you who molds contours of such a fascinating shape

A shape of deed, of doing, hope and faith
In gratitude, beauty and admired grace
Heal the poor, uplift, the sick attend
Those goodness goals on horizon to amend

Participation in nature's beauty is your deed
New momentum, show your love in which few compete
With patience, ardor and a dogged drive
Teach mankind to improve and happily so stay alive

Feast with friends, companions, cuddle, treasure
Honor and hold them close at every measure
Your fleeting, active, voyage here on earth
Gives impetus and happiness to your life's worth

We live in a never-ending conquest of Self
Too often our goals and aspirations left on the shelf
Yet faithfully follow fertile activity in our quest
Fulfill us in our deeds and doing, hope we'll pass the test

Ideas

Ideas shoot from all directions
      To measure, weigh and hold inspection

Bound to hit something, somehow
      A tree, a deer or even a cow

It's yours to choose: in which to partake?
      Or with its failures expose you as a fake

You Can Do It!

Stop stewing
Get up, do your doing

Generate energy
Spin your top
Break the spell
Body jump, spirit pop

New time, new day
You can find a new way
Do it now without delay!

Like jumping into a warm splash pool
Don't be afraid
There is no rule

Rejoice, shout out loud!
Flail hands and
Stand up tall and proud

It's yours now, it's your decision
Your chance to transform your mission
Be not afraid
Don't rue it
You can do it

The alternative is not to live!

Optimism and positive thinking
Stimulate the identity
Thoughts of success
Often self-fulfilled
It's just the game of life.

A Decalogue of Canons For Observation In Practical Life.

1. Never put off till tomorrow what you can do today.
2. Never trouble another for what you can do yourself.
3. Never spend your money before you have it.
4. Never buy what you do not want; because it is cheap, it will not necessarily be dear to you.
5. Pride costs us more than hunger, thirst, and cold.
6. We never repent of having eaten too little.
7. Nothing is troublesome that we do willingly.
8. How much pain have cost us the evils which have never happened.
9. Take things always by their smooth handle.
10. When angry, count ten, before you speak; if very angry, a hundred.

Quote from Jon Meacham's book, "Thomas Jefferson: The Art of Power"

Life for all of us is brief
Days wanted, stolen like a thief
It's up to you and me
To fill each day with worth and glee
Find happiness and inner satisfaction
For how we spend this day
Is our choice – our own election

Living Memorial Sculpture Garden,
Weed, Northern California

I CRY NO MORE

I cry no more, those wet salty tears
I said I'll try to cry no more
Live a lovely parade of parody
Humorous, unexpected feasts still ahead
Siren of love and bodily wants roar and ring
So why should I cry?

Instead, my humble body seriously celebrates
Each day, so welcome, like each pendant on a gold chain
Sparkles, rings, amuses, entices
Kindles kind, warm flames in my heart
I enjoy the solace, the secret silence, or the noisy fanfare
Like a prophet from afar, I cross over the landscape of time

I see the cracks and fissures of a lively terrain
Drawn to the horizon beyond the sun-down mountain
Good, bad, evil, beauty, mistakes
All meander from time to time in the distant past
Blown up, irrationally, as a guilty curtain, only to evaporate again

I cry no more
Not now at least!

Aspire

If you aspire,
But don't tire,
My envy, jealousy, and ire
From those who dream
But do not seem
Until they act,
To be exact.

The maker, doer,
Open, more honest, truer,
Is proud of the polished or unpolished
Products that shine,
For all to witness, criticize each line.

Once done, the act, more need,
The value is in the doing and the deed,
Let your creative juices flow
Full, free as only you will know
Regroup, you cannot please every fan,
And start anew

To create and shape again.

You'll survive when
times are tough
Of course you have to
live long enough

The author in front of the
Golden Gate Bridge, CA

Winner

Why Me?
Why Me?
I do my chores and duty to sustain
When urged to supersede, to dominate, mostly in vain
Be number one, top of the heap
Pushed off from a sorry height, fatigued and beat
Did I say imbalance?
Why Me?

So with planning and courage, I must attack
Jump up and down on my competitor's back
Fight for recognition and some success
Only to extract myself, ooze gradually out of this mess
Why Me?

But the abject hero (me) again defeated
Better strategy and muscles needed
My ego and image shrunk to midget size,
Failure into action, I again arise.
Why Me?

So, without brain nor brawn,
I do entertain a new venture
Where free spirits stay free, without negative censure
Where everyone dares and no one loses or is a sinner
An illusionary bunch where each of us is now a winner!
Did I say imbalance?

≈ ≈ ≈

We are all insecure in one way or the other.
Mother, where are you?

Some will do anything to avoid their self-image

chapter nine: no alternative to aging (yet)

"Give It Back"

"Give it back!" I cry in despair. "Give me back those rich, roaring, ripe years of indolent, dreamy youth!" Restore those delicious feelings of desire, the positive spirit of all that is possible, no worries about the future, just too much love, jive, gadgets, learning, tastes of new experiences.

No time for hoping – reality was HERE! No time for wishing for your goals, you worked, and surely would receive your just rewards. "Ah, give me back those foolish, forlorn most unbelievable dreams."

We had many aspirations, we had energy and time. We were flying in some wonderful cartoon animation with all the possibilities ahead of us. The world was OURS. The world was US. Yet, satiated, grateful, I still enjoy life.

The old bones, the back, the knees make me wince at times. Memory and recent recall fades. Yet, one look outside; trees, sky, sunbeams and my heart jumps, reveling. After all, I had my ride, my opportunities, and must accept the NOW. My eyes behold beauty constantly, my insides beat to the music of my time. The germ of youth still burns at times.

Yes, I am a busy, thankful survivor, ready to accept the day's bounty.

In my old age I met an old friend
So I knew we were still alive

Biopsy

Dear doctor,
You are well schooled, but lack a sense of humor
Do I have a growth, or an ugly tumor?
Please examine this biopsy, who knows...
Will it be fatal as it grows?
For days I waited for the result
Joined a church and joined a cult
I'd better wish, I'd better pray
Soon I may not have the time of day
Phone call claims, "It's benign
Take an aspirin and you'll be fine"

～～～

Epitaph

At the flea market
Amply displayed
Are all the knick-knacks
And junk, in awkward condition
That took me a lifetime
To collect, my tinny treasures
Discarded now, ungraciously
For a fast buck

From perfect parody of
A virtuous past
A lying, lousy bitch
Transforms at last
What was a statuesque
Beauty before
Now dying, shriveled
Lives no more

After I died.

Don't Age!

As you get older, hard to bend
The body slower nears the end
Still, senses keen, clever sensation
But mostly little things give elation

Too lazily; get up a bit late
A sparse but healthy breakfast made
To watch others bustle, ever busy
With advertising, wars, to make you dizzy

Observe the beauty of dark clouds and rain
Know nature's cycle will repeat again
Everywhere new invention and new tools
And mankind's wisdom matched by fools

To age is so inevitable, evolution, little choice
Just reminisce to adolescence, innocence of boys
Earn and learn wisdom with more contemplation
While sadly future lifeline is now on shortest ration

Years Blaze By

The years blaze by
Like a racehorse on the track
Round and round
Birthday after Birthday
To accolades and candles
Until all the candles
Do not fit anymore

～～～

You either wake up or you don't
Either way, someone has a problem to deal with

A Generation

1.

Too often
when all goes smoothly
an unexpected wrinkle
shows that imperfection is possible
tangible, ubiquitous
so simple to remove the wrinkle
but
that would change the scenery.

2.

The ROARS of planes

```
              c

   t                    i

n           the          r

e         globe        c

   v                 u

        m

                              and the noise
d     r     o     n     e     s
and awakens peaceful civilizations.
```

3.

When you are old
it's harder to

```
b
  e
    n
      d
            d
              o
                w
                  n
even though the shrunken body
                              is closer to the earth.
```

Come Listen to Me

Come listen to me
You know much
I know much
You care, I care
Now what's the problem?
So let us share

Your youth, new ideas
My wisdom –
Yes, I've been there
Done this, done that
All better after having fed
Easily said, Why not act?

I know a good laugh
Stick out neck like giraffe
I feel the sun's rays burn my arm
Innocently bolster the tan, slight alarm
I hear the baby's giggle, smile and cry
I know pain – or to be hungry by and by

Too bad; long, loving friends now departed
Close loving friendships long ago I started
My fragile body not so young anymore
Takes some effort and cosmetics now to score
Surprises, pills, treatments, medicine
Still robust, active, keep my body clean

I pontificate, I do not have to pretend
Doomsday wishers tell me it's the end
For years I've disavowed and fooled
Their dismal appetite now cooled

94

I can still choose: Say do or don't like
And if annoyed tell them to take a hike
Or I retreat to my own nest
Each day a gift, still feel blessed

Hope it will be a long time before I go
In the meantime, friendship nourishes and grows
And with my honey most endeared to care
With tons of love and kisses which we share

~ ~ ~

I believe things will grow, bear fruit,
Wither and return to earth.
Including you -
Sorry about that.

Hour Hand Too Fast

The second hand of the clock
moves so steadily in its circular route

Minute by minute
Hour by hour

While my years
Like birthdays spin happily

The old adage
Time will tell!

Doesn't it tell you too?

The best ideas are yet to come
That is why I am always waiting

Tell Me About Your Past

Tell me about your past – please!
Rancorous, into this inquisition hurled
Not to answer – so long ago – that was another world
The questionable period so vivid, yet so crass
The iron gates of mind, immutable, bad memories must pass
Answer unavailable – just now, the curtain down

Between the sunshine of the past
Journey of agony and pain, time flashes fast
The recesses of the mind picture pleasure
Wealth of love, toys, abundance, laughter in measures
Until the Hitler lightning struck

In tailspin, money spent, all goods lost,
Isolation, orphanage, hunger, fear, at any cost
6 months of loneliness, uncertainty, chilled, cold
And I was but a skinny, docile 10 year old
Cooped up with 12 other boys in a dormitory room

Reluctant – so you still want to know?
The busy mind flutters (from thought to thought), blow by blow
From place to place – the two wheeled scooter, the play puppets
Crayons, picture books
Conjecturing – collecting snails, bugs – anything that moves
Into the match boxes in my dresser drawer thrown

Rumble of relatives escaped, disappeared
My father underground – to Italy I hear
Lost my home – now sleep on the porch of a friend
Still the nature walks, the city pavement, never ends
Always active – reading the encyclopedia, ramblings of war

Ah, the power not to share yet, to hold within
Special delicacies made by mother and the next of kin
Grandma counting out 10 raisins in bed at nighttime
Knee deep in grass or over fences I do climb
To the counter – ten Pfenning worth of lakritze

As thoughts do percolate seemingly so real, so bereft
Homesick, lonely, only one friend, Justus, left
Talk of going far away to America – alone
Impossible to shut out goodness, innocent
Nothing to atone

No, can't you see – I am not ready to answer you yet.
I packed a special carton full of toys, games, books, clothing
Just in case
I did this at age 9 – ready to escape the chase
But my mother sold the box, moved me onto a friend's porch

It was 18 months of waiting until my visa to see Liberty's torch
By then I was 12
So in time, patience – when can I figure it all out?
Digest, reconstruct, matriculate, and once again be proud?
Home, earth, street air – all so special then – no more

An avalanche of thoughts come to surface – too wounded to delve
I cannot bare my soul just yet!

Celebrate Now

I want to carve myself into the book of immortality
My epitaph: "Live, love and learn."

Join my dance with my soul in rhythmic splendor
Erase the agony of loneliness, hopelessness
Celebrate my life, now, in the moment
I may topple from the pinnacle of success
Thrashing into the gloom of utter despair
Only to rise again to celebrate

But what if I never reach these lofty heights?
What if I stay as "everyman" doing my thing
Work, love, rejoice in the chorus for the world
Almost gratified with what I have and have not
Simply a teacher, a businessman, a family man
Following a daily routine
Still a slave to the system in which I live
Dangling at the cliff, barely holding on

Best now to let go, fall into the icy water below
Swim in the torturous stream of humanity
Then quickly dry
They say an angel saved me
I can barely appreciate the magnificence of the scenery about
Just want to return home to warmth and comfort
Someone filmed my fall, scattered it on the Internet
Live in the flick, in time set

Who wants immortality anyhow, after it's over?

Heartbeat

I cherish, am thrilled - unaware of my thumping **heartbeat!**
This is my moment, my diamond
Not to wear or spare,
But to feel within
Exulted power of omnipotence and happiness
Of body's delight
Merged in the pleasant, the good, the beautiful,
Sense dramatically, all rolled into one
Simultaneous!
All tentacles, all feeling, alert
Live alert as I radiate my six senses
Immersed in life's sensations

Within - I sing silent and loud
I share the living world!
I must be here
For me - for you - for all mankind
For I do love the sun's warm rays
I love my friends. I love you!

Yes, my son – aged, I feel well
Were God to extinguish my last breath soon
I'd shout that this, and every moment, is **the greatest**
Allowed by the majestic divinity

Author with wife Lillian
and baby Jeff

Climb Mountains

How many **twice 43-year olds** do you know,
Still dreamers, schemers and believers?
Who built our world, lauded mankind
Calmed the excesses of the younger generation
Found treasures in nature's beauty
Fascinated by inventions, new reasoning
And modern methods
Still optimistic that peace is around the corner
A brittle, dwindling people
Full of hormones and physical conquests
Energetic, alive, vibrant
Ready to mesmerize and romance the ladies
Ready to climb mountains
Maybe only one at a time
Slow, deliberate
Wonderful, happy in spite of tragedy about
Waiting for the wonder of tomorrow

You Are Old

You who are mighty, profound
Style up knowledge by the pound
Command creators
No small potatoes
Slip and show
Bathe in your alter ego
Sceptre over your firm head
Figuratively foolish, funny phantom stories fed
Adulated, adored, admired
Frown, feared, fortunate
But much desired
But you are old
and I am not
and
I wouldn't trade
for a thousand pounds of pot

chapter ten: nonsense!

Nonsense

Except for you or me, much conversation borders on nonsense. After all, when my kids were babies, having not learned much vocabulary, they blurted out babbling nonsense. So I, in turn, articulated some story about an elephant and a camel who, in collusion, planned to escape from their zoo. I forgot that an elephant and camel can't read roadmaps, and after all, in winter, where would they go since hay is not readily available as it was in the zoo. All utter nonsense!

And that in turn, of course, brings to mind all the politicians voting on hundreds of prospective laws that they have not read, resulting in much confusion, restriction and above all, total nonsense. Even rich millionaires have periods when their activities relate to nonsense and their reputations as being erudite proves a misnomer. And yet in this tense, stressful world, we do all need some relief, some inane humor, some escape from the ritual daily routine when we are not only faced with the nonsense of the world, but actually have to partake in it.

Careful if your form of nonsense is debilitating, wasteful, unhealthy or stupid. On the contrary, we actually partake in useful nonsense every day. The way we talk to our dogs and cats, daydream, and tell the most creative nonsensical stories as matter of fact. Think of how frugal and careful you are, yet daily and weekly you squander away countless hours. You say that is nonsense? So be it! Often the best fairy tales, jokes and humor are portrayed as nonsense, while it livens up our senses of humor and thinking.

Since everyday activities, our occupations, studies, readings and physical exercise are all pertinent to healthy living, there is so little time for nonsense! Ever so often we escape on a vacation to relieve pressure, relax, travel and be free spirited, simply bathing in nonsense.

Of course if you read a book, swim in a pool, make love, these are far from nonsense. Best get to the point of fruition, action, than overcome a mountain of obstacles; most of them are nonsense. And bragging about your heroism is also nonsense.

So if you read and partake in much nonsense I would consider you a normal, balanced person.

And of course that too is nonsense.

We think we are
We are we think

Rave and Rant

Search my pockets, search my pants
Won't find nothin', not even ants
Raves and rants
Grow up please, make some sense

Somewhere there's a foolish war
Misjudged, rotten to the core
Sore on, Bore on, Tore on
After and before on

So I'm a blank
Barely fear the hand grenade or tank
Broach the ocean
Without notion

You don't have to be
so bright
Just to switch on the
light
and see all
before you

Still the pill and swallow potion
Pizzazz out
Turn about
Crawl back in my shell

Inhibitions shattered well
I curse, I cajole with candor craze
Reflections torturous in my face
It's all wrong, time and place

This far away combat to protect
Stave off enemy, show respect
Now I too rave and rant
I do not understand, I do not understand

*Every time you get something for nothing,
you pay a price*

If No Calendar, Cat or Ladder

First day a superstition
Black cat out front
Now your decision

Under a ladder is not safe
Sometimes slips and won't behave
If no ladder is on your way
No complaint, not a thing to say

Now if no calendar is in place
13th day you'll never face
If no cat ran out in front of road
You'd be home and sow your oats

Salt over left shoulder
Was anyone looking?
No, then all is OK
So knock on wood!

I bought a back-
scratcher for 99 cents.
A most ticklish bargain

Can You?

Polish, shine the shoes
Quickly scan the latest news
Plant a tomato, watch it grow
Fun to reap what you can sow

Assemble and create
Season the full plate
Make some eggs
Study her legs

Wash the car
Busy by far, be a star
Relax, rest, take a cure
Save some dough, don't be poor

But I can think, and feel
And dream and love so personal and real
And laugh and cry
But sometimes don't know why

Not so sure and often second-guessed
Within myself I am obsessed
Can you? Can try, can do
Can die, not you

We all will, that's true
So plan to participate
Do it today, before it is too late

Divide the difference
Between the human race
Come up with people with emotions,
Feelings and will

Irritants

There are always irritants
Human or otherwise
That bug us, keep us alert
Try to dominate
The trick is to blow them away
With kindness

Virginity Lost

Virgin soil, Virgin Airlines
Virgin Records
Virginity once prized
Once experienced
Open new world
Open world
Out of the virgin womb
Ideas and empires born
She lost her virginity long ago!
Still Elizabeth was a famous queen

Google is Not God

Some answers Google does not have!
"Does she love me?"
"Will I be alive tomorrow, after the next revolution of the earth?"
"Will the moon's gravity suddenly decrease?"
"When will the next tsunami, earthquake occur?"
"Which great person will die next week?"
No, Google is not God
And life's little surprises had better be left for tomorrow.

My bed in the morning looks like I slept in it

Discard Clothing Uninhibited

Ponderous discard my pants, engage each leg
Elevate up staircase step by step
An eerie sense of liberty instills
Cast off my clothes, a dream fulfills

Like cavemen, bodies, in their flesh
Escape pupa with nature now must clash
Labor of love duty, I work downstairs
Yet upstairs are my new affairs

Strip all, stark naked full of zest
Fatigued, half-sleep doze now in self arrest
So clear, clairvoyant try to break away
Fully liberated like free bird this end of day

Sans cloth, sans everything
In privacy upstairs in my own ring
Spirit free the likes of a three year old
I gallivanted, rejoiced, so mighty and so bold

I jump, I strut, I stretch a lot
Crawl on all fours like a jolly mutt
Body erect in exposition stand
Smile, fool ego that I seem quite grand

Derisive shrill ring of my door bell: "I'm in shock!"
In front of mirror without stich of cloth or frock
Hurriedly must dress, rejoin the race
And lose myself just like another disappearing face

Some days I can see so clearly
That I excite my inner feelings
I solve mental puzzles and I know
It will all be alright

Who Cares?

Tired, mired
Not admired
Who cares?

Resigned, find
Seldom dined
Who cares?

Passionate feelings
Rejection, reeling
Who cares?

Wallet blank
Don't thank
Who cares?

Letter praised
Check or raise
Who cares?

Piedmont 4th July Parade, CA 2012

Model and hunk
Muscles first rung
Who cares?

Ten thousand flies
Ten thousand lies
Who cares?

Beggar asked,
"Please give,
Just want to live"
Who cares?

Overeat and overspend
No, money simply can't mend
Who cares?

THE END

I Got Scalped

Barber in angry mood,
Decimated and raped my head.
Four months of growth,
Brownish silver soft hair
On the linoleum floor, dead.

My hair!
"No, no," I muttered,
But it was too late.

He had to balance sides,
Even the remaining strands of hair.
God given, wavy, proud
Why did I ever go here?
And now I have to pay for the insult.

I think I'll hide for two or three months,
Wear a wig or hat,
Or tell them I shall act in
The next grotesque comedy.

Night Table

My night table is crammed
Sometimes my life feels damned
Glasses, pens, pills and paper
Like my inner soul in a caper
Upside down
Should I escape, get out of town?
And I forgot to write my will

April Fool

Keep your cool
It's an April fool
Spring has sprung
The lark has sung
You simply smile and hold your tongue

April fool
Sit on the stool
You've got one ear a different size
Glance down and you may realize
Your body's not yet ready for a prize

April fool
Reborn, rejuvenated, with new rule
The year just ended has but started
Ice cold, frozen drifts have parted
The return of hope in spring expected

April fool
With hope and sun
Hopeful predictions, frolic, fun
Yet share with school, duties and with work
Yet time for courting, loving is our perk

April fool
All is just make-believe
My parents' nagging mellowed to reprieve
If I can only win the race, catch a ball or join the chase
I'll know I am lucky in this phase

~ ~ ~

I knew I couldn't do it
That's why I did it
And I was right!

Wringing Out The Mind

when we wring out the mind
always another
drop   of wisdom

slowdown
                    patience
be honest
with thyself

the orange   FULLY squeeeezed
                              The towel stopped

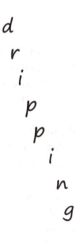

d
r
 i
  p
   p
    i
     n
      g

the mind says
        make this a healthy delicious me
the mind says
        help!   and really means it
    deny the mind
                follow the mind

chapter eleven: trust and faith

Trust and Faith

A wonderful small room in a luxury apartment: bed, dresser, and most of all toys and books, the room I lived in, mine for the last eight years. To my nine year old self this was part of what I trusted, my security blanket. Most cherished of all was my toy front façade of a puppet theater with a tiny curtain and thirty-five or so puppets, like the king with golden crown, his queen, many knights and of course the crocodile.

"What's this got to do with the beans of Boston?" you ask. Simply this; I was in Hanover, Germany during Hitler's reign around 1935-36. One day, my mother sent me to an old couple with a two bedroom apartment at the other side of town. Tante Adele and Uncle Arnold were like foster parents to me. That late afternoon, my mother came to their apartment to pick me up.

"Well, it's all gone." She had auctioned off the entire apartment: library, paintings, oriental rugs and, of course, my room - books, puppets and all. In a box, she brought me four remaining puppets and three books, including James Fennimore Cooper, Leatherstocking Tales, all, of course, in German. Now, unfortunately, all lost.

Next, my dad, whom I rarely saw, who was a successful travelling salesmen, escorted me on the train eight hours from my only home and dropped me off at an orphanage on the hill in Esslinger. He said good bye, and escaped to Italy. Again shocked, crying at times, despite the good care and camaraderie of the other boys, I felt abandoned and was homesick for the first six months.

After waiting for two years, in August 1938 my mother brought me from Hanover to Hamburg Harbor by train. I joined fourteen other youngsters to go to New York on a boat, never to return, with my mother saying a tearful good bye.

"Did you lose faith, trust?" you may well ask. A bit of insecurity, yes! You see, trust was imbedded in my being, just like honesty, faith and blind hope. It was my mother's upbringing, my community, cherished value and morals. Like the snail carries its house, so forever I will cherish these values, part of the morals with which I was brought up. Many times in later life I was lied to, cheated, parted with what I thought were good friends. Even the local government laws, often unjust, unfair, biased could not sway this grounded trust in me. As I was jilted, cheated often at great cost, the tenets of truth, trust, fealty, goodness in mankind simply stayed in my mind. Sure, I became more cautious, more careful, more suspicious, but deep down I believed in the value of trust.

Well, from utter poverty to serving in the U.S. Army, to teaching for twenty-five years, most contacts have proven true and trustworthy: my grown children, my deceased wife (married for forty-four years). I lived in a 5900 square foot mansion for twenty-four years in one of the best little cities, climates and schools in all the U.S., and this could not have happened if others had not trusted in me as I trusted in them. Sure, all the disappointments and expectations wore heavily on me. Yet, the good far outdid the bad and my love of life, family, people, and my strong foundation from youth continues to be my shield and my strength in retaining inner happiness ever-lasting.

Trust

Trust is a precious commodity
To break it, tragic oddity
The temptation to over-talk
Hesitate, reveal and balk
Spill the beans, undermine
Word of mouth, grief and whine
Should I let the secret out of the bag?
Open wound with filthy rag?

That inner see-saw song
The right and wrong
We meddle, we cheat
When there is no need
Or even if tempted - say no
Be straight as an arrow - no show
Trust if you must
Or reputation bust

A pivotal life may hang in balance
Trust is far more than taking a chance
Trust is a friend
Trust is a lover on whom you depend
Trust is the inner fabric, if you must
Value to belief and inner lust

Once trust is broken
Mistrust and doubt there is no joking
It is a let-down, disappointment
A wound, almost dismemberment
No more friends if you fail to trust
Broken - bonds, telltale bust

∾ ∾ ∾

It's easy to say I'm sorry
But harder to mean it

Living Memorial Sculpture Garden,
Weed, Northern California

111

I See Through People

Sometimes
   my eyes
      see through people
Into their hearts and inner beings
A spiritual, uplifting experience
Absorb their concern and torment
Joy and fear
Anguish, pain, concern

In empathy, transfer the vibes into my being
Indeed we are all so fragile, so brittle
Yet often strong, solid on the inside
Prick into the skin, humanity will ooze out
A different kind of Superman

No time to analyze their brains
Weigh their moods
Listen, smell, learn their ways
Perhaps advise, or soothe
Listen and
    listen more
      eye to eye
But I have no such psychic powers
Let me tolerate their imperfections
As they too, tolerate mine

And maybe, just maybe, I'll make a friend or two!

*Piedmont 4th
July Parade,
CA 2012*

Relationships

Every relationship, like an ocean ship,
Has ups and downs, rises and dips
The subservient or dominant character relents
A constant contest between two never ends
The id rises and proclaims: Respect me!
I'm a person too, can't you see?

Often roles may change
As "his and her" relationship does rearrange
So close, if they only knew
Love and trust the ever-binding glue

Two unique individuals cemented
Their past and present now presented
They must learn to adjust
Ego and id are refined in trust
Patience, tolerance, be kind or bust
Avoid quick decisions followed by apologetic remorse
May end in disappointment or the threat of divorce

Let change and challenge follow
A new gentle wind does blow
In partnership do reap what they did sow
We need expanding, and broad vision
As thought and will to merge bring new decisions
Out of heavy fermentation, a happier brew
Isn't it time to recreate the love you knew?

Sing then in unison a harmonious tune
Start now, the time can never be too soon!

～ ～ ～

Stay strong and firm in your conviction
But if you break the trust then all is fiction

Necessary Woman

Woman's electric power ignites
The iron curtain alights
Bursts open the glass ceiling
Shattering into sparkling pieces, reeling
To a new enlightened day, foreseeing
Dawning into a crescendo of crackling proportion
Yet her hidden magic power spells care and caution

Compliments, voices influence
Pervasive perhaps, direct affluence
Feminine powers now unleashed
"We bore your child," they say, unabashed
"We teach, instill your values every day!"
Our skills and talents everywhere to compliment
Not just child but human values we defend

Our every effort to grow human seed
To join the underdog, the sick and aged in need
Together – family, we mold
New leaders, entrepreneurs, injustices sold
Too long our talents were ignored
It's time now that women scored
Our feelings, desires priceless treasures
With love devotion who can measure?
Now we women bloom in open, fresh air
New dawn of hope and faith show we damn right care

The time is ripe – the time is right!
We are your companions and your guides
God made us different, gave us duress
In this difference emerges our uniqueness
Our beauty, our love, our soul
We are your partners, we make you whole
Accept our precious lot
We're here to stay, like it or not!

She Clouds My Mind

Stop it!
I told my mind
So constantly bound by her
Her silhouette fixed in mind
Thoughts, feelings,
Inflicted on me
As if doped all in dreamland to her
As if
We two would be together
When we are really far apart
Even when I pray
She clouds my mind
As I return to full bloom
Flower - lovely gentle.
An apparition or maybe real
Once so wonderful
Now so uncertain
A touch of agony
Can you feel my pain?

≈≈≈

Even the rules of law are portrayed differently
by different societies
That is why what is yours is NOT mine
But you think mine is yours...

Nine Lives

Sensitive, perceptive
To your passionate partner
Open-eyed, not blind
Respond in kind
But remember your battery
Has only nine lives

Cost more than nickel
Woman so jolly and fickle
So lovely and close
Wrong word then verbose
We love and hate
Entwined and too late

While love and earth spin
Delicious pickle we're in
Wouldn't trade
Until too late
Revenge and acrimony our new fate
So our curdled blood
Like it or not!

~ ~ ~

Lots of trivia leads to lots more trivia
So what could be so important?

I can see through you and your antics
and I don't need glasses
to do so

A Lafayette, CA Middle School poetry talk, 2012

The Fray

Sometimes it's wise to jump in the fray
Of course not every day
Small risk, large prize
Toe in the water such a surprise

And if you're on the winning side
Stubborn strength the fight is right
I would have liked a helping hand
Sadly I made a mess of it, you understand

≈ ≈ ≈

Shall I forgive and forget?
I search my soul - but it is a false forgiveness

117

chapter twelve: war, war, war

This is an imaginary poem, but it could have been Anne Frank on her way to Auschwitz Concentration Camp.

Lieselotte

Lieselotte snapped out of her slumber
The nine year old, petite, precocious girl,
Crammed next to Mutti in this stinking cattle car.
The cramped humanity, barely room to sit or lie,
Clothes for three days, no latrine
Old, sick, coughing, indigent
Several had died already as the wagons moved on.
Ever so often they would open up the rolling doors
Somewhere in the country.
Always the uniformed, angry guards
With their rifles, guns, dogs, harsh commands
They said "On the way to the East, Poland!"
The sad, eerie sound of wailing, whining,
The endurance of pain - all but mesmerized
The clatter of the railroad wheels below ever moving.

It was barely fourteen months ago,
Their beautiful large apartment in Berlin
Oriental carpets, book cases with leather bound books
Lots of oil paintings adorned the walls,
An upright piano festooned with music pamphlets
Mutti was a great pianist, she even sang,
And dad, a physician, a skin specialist
Enjoyed a large well-earned practice.
"My room," Lieselotte half dreamt and recalled,
"Had my own wardrobe, a small bookcase,
A wonderful collection of dolls
A clown picture on the wall.
And even a large dollhouse that Vati gave me at Chanukah.
During the holidays aunts and uncles would visit
And Ursula my best friend would laugh and make up droll stories.
But all that was before!"
The clatter of the railroad wheels below ever moving.

One day Mutti said, "You must go to a Jewish day school,
That's a rule and new law.
Vati can't practice at the hospital nor treat non-Jewish patients.
Not allowed to go to the Kino, the movies
To the children's matinee on Saturday,
Or play with the other kids outside.
Our maid Justine had to be let go."
Many friends left for the United States or Palestine,
or South America - things were getting ugly.
The raucous preaching by Hitler or Goebbels, or Goering
Drowned out any privacy.

The clatter of the railroad wheels below ever moving.

One day, on short order: "Must sell everything
And meet at the Marketplace with one suitcase each."
They say the law is the law.
"Pappi always taught me to be honest and obedient
And so I reluctantly went along.
Our apartment was auctioned off in one day
And now we are headed to the Ghetto in Warsaw,
Everywhere there was poverty, hunger, stern faces.
What did we do? We were all so innocent and overwrought."

The clatter of the railroad wheels below ever moving.

"Was it my fault that my parents were born Jewish
And taught me the ten commandments as best they could?
I must cover my ears", Lieselotte thought.
"I must close my eyes and think of good things,
Birthday parties, Friday evening dinner with the Sabbath candles,
Vacation at the Ostsee at Nordernei.
I must hope again ready for a festive meal."
But Lieselotte's short life, little did she know,
Was coming to an end. Would it end soon?
After weeks of starvation and deprivation, huddled in Warsaw,
The family was broken up.

The clatter of the railroad wheels below ever moving.

One day they were lined up again,
Suitcase filled with what was left.
And so now she is in the jammed cars of cattle wagons ready for
Yes, ready for Auschwitz. So much prospect!
So much hope! All vanished under the voice of the Final Solution
The extermination of all Jews.

The clatter of the railroad wheels below ever moving.

All I can say is, "Auf Wiedersehn Lieselotte
You and one and half million other innocent
Children; victims of a mad, prejudiced society.

The clatter of the railroad wheels ceased.

Essay BUZZBOMB

I wrote this in June of 1945 when 50,000 American prisoners of war were suddenly freed with the German collapse and flown to an obscure tent city for 20,000 people called Lucky Strike (after the cigarettes), near Rouen, France. I was shipped there from Liege, our combat Engineer Base, as a temporary clerk helper for three weeks, then recalled to my unit, which was ready to fight the Japanese who still engaged us in WWII. Buzzbomb was a real fuzzy, friendly mutt, a terrier.

"Buzz-Bomb," I yelled. Soon before me stood the little creature with its long wiggling tail, and those gleaming eyes. Buzz-Bomb was a cute little brown pup we had picked up during the early stages of the V-I and V-II raids on London. While we were in the Midlands near Shrewsbury building Baily bridges and in the heart of London during the Buzz bomb raids, the dog had grown up with us, the pride of our company. He had followed us during training, lived and slept in out tents, ate our chow, and only differed from a soldier in that he never barked back. By the time we crossed the channel on the LST, Buzz-Bomb was considered a traveling dog. He had two exceptional qualities, one being that he would run away, but always return. The other occurred at night. He was watchful and would loudly bark at strangers coming nearby. It was during those wet, stalling days in December, near the German border that Buzz-Bomb made a name
120

for himself. We had just arrived and our company split into three platoons. Our position was near a deserted, shot-up, abandoned village. Since there was not much activity, we only had two guards out, the Front being several miles away. The time was just before the Battle of the Bulge when the Wermacht, stretched to the last effort, started the counter offensive.

German patrols and fifth-columnists, aided by paratroopers, infiltrated into our lines, caught many units off guard, and at the time captured many men, including valuable booty. We were weary from the day's fatigue, and with the exception of the guards, everyone was fast asleep.

All of a sudden, in the pitch darkness, there was a sudden, loud bark. We all awoke and by natural instinct reached for our guns, while some of us held our pistols ready. Under orders from the lieutenant, we quietly slipped away. It was useless to fight a foe that we could not see. One of our guards was missing and the action seemed to be much closer. No sooner had we taken the first step back when the dog began to bark, warning us. We must have been only a hundred yards away. Than a loud BANG! A yelp. They had shot our dog. We knew now where their location was. We reached our unit, informed the C.O. and soon came orders for a temporary retreat.

We had been saved from whatever the Jerries had planned for us by the poor dog. Never shall I forget the warning bark of Buzz-Bomb, who for once in his life never returned.

Man is quite sophisticated and knowledgeable today
But our stupid stubborn egos get us into intolerable wars

≈ ≈ ≈

Attention!

(I actually observed this several times during inspection while serving in the U.S. Army in World War II. Much later, I wrote the poem "Fainting Guard" on the facing page.)

Today is inspection day, in O.D.'s on the parade ground. It is a very hot, humid day. Stern, stoic, tough, blatant. The trumpets blare. The garrulous guards, the soldiers, all stand at attention. The medaled general inspects the colors. Cautious, critical, determined. The honorable, erect guard shouts, "Present arms!" an icy command.

Instinctively, the troops obey the order. Haven't they stood in the unbearable heat long enough? Just as the general passes, one guard faints. Like a rock, he collapses from common heatstroke. Falls to the ground like a sack, seemingly dead. Drops his rifle, all; out cold! No one dares to look or help...

The general parades by, alertly looking each soldier in the eye as if nothing has happened. Discipline comes first!

Fainting Guard

Full dress inspection time!
Three platoons
Company A- tten- tion!
A hot and humid day
Stern, stoic, tough
Trumpets blare

Guards stand to attention
General inspects colors
Critical — determined
Honor guard commands
Pre- sent arms!

Just as the general passes
One guard man faints
Rifle clattering
No one dares look or help him
The general moves on
As though nothing happened
The body still collapsed on ground

Nothing happened

Discipline comes first
What is a soldier's life worth anyhow?

This is how wars are won

GOOD-BYE

Singular, he lifted his daughter tenderly
Into a bundle, hugged and kissed her,
Cheek upon cheek, warmth,
The elemental paternal love
A momentary binding
One in innocence receive love,
The other more conscious,
Tight, but not too tight.

He slowly lowered her to the floor,
They looked at each-other;
"Good-bye,"
"Good-bye, Daddy,"
A tearful kiss and long embrace with his
Beautiful wife

And with that
He took his satchel and
duffel bag,
    turned around

        and took

the   train

    to save
America.

Arthur Weil

124

The Veteran

Pity the poor slob
Who waddles like a dragged dog
Head bowed to the pavement
A gray, jagged, fatigued, worn-out olive-colored jacket
Unkempt, weather-beaten, a comical caricature
Performs like an uphill skier
Peers a few feet ahead

Maybe, just maybe, years ago in uniform for us
Tail waggles no more, in ignorance, nor euphoric happiness
Shed his human values, dignity lost
Decimated, beaten, succumbed, downtrodden
His haven and home long ago not accommodating
The free spirit broken with disease, lethargy, drugs
Yes, he served years – the veteran

Rejected most help, love lost long ago
Now just a replica in the mirror of a puddle
Degradation, stagnation, self-affliction
All encompassed in this hull of a creature
Mumbling, incoherent, yet precariously
Slugging it out like a drunkard finding his uneven course
We know why! We know when!
He was an honored veteran once, but lost his way
And much more

∼ ∼ ∼

He fought on the wrong side
Landed in the wrong grave

He who dares gets ahead faster
(or dies sooner)

125

The Pain

You will never feel my pain
                    Nor I yours
Commiserate, sympathize, yes
This life battle is not my choice
Our dear ones on foreign shores
Despite the bulletproof vest, the plated armor
Remote explosions, snipers, wounded
Even an allied soldier turns; goes crazy
War has glued our painful souls

Wily, well-equipped trained combatants
For some cause or other, men will kill
In dark sadness, hopelessness
Explosions, dead and wounded
                        Innocent
Blind hatred engulfs the antagonists
While curtains are closed
Doors are sealed
All waiting for the unexpected

Yet, we bond with our partners
Bind with warm family and friends
In a spirit of a new light
Though my pain diminishes
                        It is real!
Like a healed broken member
In time, frolic and laughter
First fighting and last armistice
So changed, miles apart

Rebuild, those who return
Somewhere there is a better world and I will find it

        and forget
                    the Pain

Living Memorial Sculpture Garden, Weed, Northern California

IN HIDING

Brash, boisterous, almost barbaric
He stormed into the room, a tyrant provocateur
Demanded obedience, loyalty

"Where is the girl?"

Silence and fear wreaked havoc
Testosterone reached its zenith
"Produce the woman, now"
The demand, cold and icy
Threw more fear into the crowd

"Where is she hiding?"

Shudder… but no!
Below the floor boards in the attic...

But Mum's the word
Some dare risk all

The Egotistic Commander

Lubricate words and massage the soul
Dagger to the ventricle to still the demons
For hideous hell haunts and taunts
But you overstepped, used power unwisely

How will spirit ever reach your brain?
You, the commander who ordered a direct missile
Result: more cold, callous killings
Despite the medals, your earned army bars

No direction, no cursive note, no messianic message
Errors, wrong judgment, precious civilian lives lost, wasted
You, the sincere saint, should be the great guardian of sanity
Instead the gruesome, dangerous dispatcher of dead
Destruction wrapped in seniority and secret duty
A conflagration, a foul fire, a convenient cry for retaliation

Thus, your foolish folly in ever ego-ridden self-glorification
Has born that deadly fruit we always feared
Mass bolstered burial is tomorrow
The wailing and howling cries
Followed by gun-toting men for revenge
Secret messenger with
Half-assembled rockets already dispatched
You ignited the fire.

As planes loaded with soldiers head in our direction
All your missile interference will not dissuade
The brain-washed, bitter, brash armada headed our way
Without foresight, simply to kill, you dared to direct
Broke protocol and all apologies are for naught
Armageddon is on its way.

No, you can't use atomic devices
Unless self-destruction and desolation
Of your own is your desire
Better heed the laws of nature, reason and caution
The advancing enemy is full of venom, hate and revenge

They have discarded pity, love, and kindness long ago
The word forgiveness is not in their vocabulary
Only a natural calamity will stop them

Go, follow your archaic, ancient rules of self defense
Sacrificing all.
One error and all is for naught!
The souls of spilled blood
The maimed and wounded will cry out
Remember triumph will find its own justice
And maybe, just maybe
Mankind will return to decency, humanity
Learn to live in tolerance and peace

Freedom Flag Flutters

The screw is tightened wrench by wrench
A national armed camp of self-defense
Our liberties diminished are no match
A bloody war empties the till and often makes no sense

We bragged as mightiest, greatest nation, just the best
With latest most sophisticated weapons to defend our shores
The bigoted, evil outside world now put us to the test
But whom to fight which deafened by the lion's roars

Our civil rights abridged in face of war
Some test the chorus justifying, curtailing our constitution
We bow so meekly, protest and imprisonment abhor
The tragedy of political decay, results in seeds of revolution

Yet with 9/11 threshold of fear
Our Bill of Rights so sacred and so dear
In balance leaders do not sacrifice
Freedom flag flutters, never to be put on ice

Vast social projects now at stake
Social security for young and old
Too much borrowed, no more to take
New reconstructed way of life all told

chapter thirteen: humanity

Essay on Differences in Humanity

To be different is not easy when we all want to assimilate and belong. We want to speak differently, act differently, and think differently. There is too much misunderstanding already - but if I say "no"; no nukes, no war, no confrontation, am I so different? We all are born out of different molds, with different genes and chromosomes – yet we are not mutations, aberrations or weird creatures that no one can understand and must be obliterated! We struggle with the luck and fate of our birth and place, not by choice. It's a mobile world where civilizations merge more than ever, yet some peoples still fight for their identity, often at the deadly cost of thousands.

There is strength in our differences. The sauces taste different due to their ingredients - a touch of spice here, a few herbs there, more sugar and less salt until a delicious palatable taste is created. So two humans learn and work together to create the new and accept constructive differences.

We all love life, yet, despite customs and mores of our peoples, we are still competitive, and age too quickly from the stresses we put on ourselves. We all aspire for peace and yet we all have our own prejudices and hates. We feel helpless in a world riddled with conflict. We must begin to respect the different tongues, customs and religions of others, and not just tolerate, but understand. We do all this imbued with a zestful spirit for life, for our selves and with desire for the best for our posterity.

Ready to Take Our Place

A mystic light-like meteor
Dashed over the countryside as if to score
All were in awe
For those who witnessed and saw
Nothing stayed the same
Pear and apple trees now rotten, cows went lame
The corn turned dry and green
Famine and heat as the grass dried clean

Tree leaves too turned brown
People left, the village turned into a ghost town
For days the chickens laid no eggs
Only the caterpillars and the pests had a million legs
And the farmer's wife went into a deep depression
As if she met the spooky ghost at a dreamy session
Maybe the cosmic rays from a planetoid
Turned tables and created nature's void
Or the riveting energy from a meteor
Brought this disaster to our core

Was it a warning that another planet in outer space
Is responsible for the damage, ready to take our place?
If you don't believe, feel extreme heat and cold
Mysterious airwaves in our brain now sold
Or why we speak but no one hears
Stubbornly, "I dare you!" and nasty war appears

We Are Extreme

Some of us laggards, a brand apart
Wasteful and frivolous, don't finish what we start
Undisciplined, we forge ahead
Often contrary, end up behind instead

An extra cup of coffee or tea
Ignore the pressure warning plea
Blind to fast pace, take own time
Assume life is a ball, most sublime

We eat at our leisure
Ignore the inevitable upcoming seizure
Our dress so colorful and risqué
We're every man by night and day

We live on credit to the hilt
Oblivious that lender is ill-willed
We love, push nature to extreme
We raise our luck on devil's beam

We are the alter-ego and forbidden fruit
We demonstrate, cajole as fits our mood
We are free spirits, revolutionary game
Unless you harness us, our nation will never be the same

STORIES

Sailing, sailing at 18,000 feet
550 miles an hour
120 sardine-packed passengers
Somewhere beyond the Mississippi
Over the clouds
Infinite space
Way above the white marshmallow clouds
While sunlight glistens
10 million stories unravel down below

Which one is yours?

Face Our Own Reality

My prurient appetite
For visual flesh
Stripped nude
Lecherous, predatory
Like a female tiger in heat

The animal in all of us
Uncovered, undressed
Is but a pig, a dog
A horse, a tiger
Some with grace
Slink like a feline
Or wobble like a sow

What direction
Where to go
What do I see?
What do my eyes miss?
Are my nostrils picking up the scent?

The human sidewalks crowded
No different than animals in the zoo
Only more dressed
More covered up
More protected
Too soon starved

We gobble down
We chew, we taste
Smack our lips
The aromas to the nostril
Devour before they devour me
Appetite quenched for the moment

But eventually we all
Have to bathe and shower
And face our own reality

Fondly
Favorite
Forward
Look
Divert
Be creative
Not by the
Book
How else can we
Humankind
Integrate
Beat
Our competition
Before it's
Too late?

Why can't we be the
nation of happy,
satisfied,
contradictory,
creative
people that we are?

Nation's Self Defense

We earth people cover ourselves
Darndest clothing
Some splendid, comfortable or loathing
Some tribes wear little, mostly bare
Opposite sex so stimulated to stare
But were it not for human chemicals

There's really not much there

I Do What I Can

He said
I am
I do what I can
I cannot change the sky and sea
They are so open, blue and free

Exuberantly I play
Run, exercise without delay
Share passions, friendships and sometimes pain
Knowing after sun may come the rain

I am
I do the best I can
If I get angry I'll explode
I'll let it out not get my goat
I'll stay calm and keep my cool
Better than being called a fool

I am
I'll do the best I can
So when I feel passion for you
My hormones, testosterone ring so true
For you are close, you are my friend
You share and let our feelings blend

I am
I'll do the best I can

Concentric Circles - Where do you fit in?

Our lives spiral in concentric circles
        First you ascend, than wobble, hobble
                A glider catching tailwinds
                        So too, we drift - circle, spiral with purpose

                Always at nature's mercy
        Often rudderless in pursuit
Of fame, of wealth, of recognition
Edged on by curiosity, challenge

Always we fill up our nests with gadgets
        Phones, TV screens, and gizmos of the latest invention
                Even plan for a bigger nest to store our acquisition
                        Daring in our middle age, we still circle above

                More settled, still too busy, bustling, living
        Ignore the clock of life as it ticks to conclusion
And not yet afraid of the cosmos' last fanfare
Before it will self-destruct

We have acquired the gift of preaching tolerance
        We try to be the messengers of understanding
                Always learning anew
                        Observers of the arts, the sports, TV

                We become the spiritual creatures of hope
        Hope for our children, our posterity
We try to touch nirvana
We get involved with global issues

We introspect and ask for forgiveness
        As we fly, circle, oblong, up and down
                Seeing our own reflection on earth
                        Still busy with meals, health problems, travel

Trying to enjoy the little things
    If granted another year, there is still time left
        To join the chorus of peace
            Sit on a bench watching birds peck, dive for
            fish and insects

            A casual conversation with old friends
        Attend a movie, or concert or play
      A dish of strawberries and vanilla ice-cream
    Still alert to absorb the latest news regardless
Of consequences and have strong opinions

    So on what level and stage in the circle are you today?

Dare Me

Dare me

I, a seed of seeds from Adam ...	or before
I, alive, searching this great earth...	that I adore
I, a microcosm, grain amongst ...	mankind living
Eager to meld, wide joy...	of giving
Dare me, care for me ...	spare me

Touch me

Stir the juices, shapes	that I may thrive
Now here is my moment	my time
Echo, mold and shape	I'm in my prime
The single chain of deeds	that feeds
Work, fun and grieving...	all are meshed
Autumn harvest gathers...	shaken, thrashed
Here's to the fruit...	the loot to suit

Stray not

Disappoint me not, your seed...	now grieving
Put me on your pedestal...	forever feeling
Great in need distrust...	but still believing
Growing, growing...	maturing
Inert - feel the great grandeurs...	of life
I wonder what tomorrow brings.	

136

Braggadocio so dominant in sound
In rapture all ears listen all around
Until with gestures and great repetition
The tired audience, no more listen

As our speaker froths at the mouth
Depicts an egocentric vagabond and louse
His audience soon melts and disappears
He still pontificates, drowns in his own tears

Soon word spreads among the citizens in town
At sound of B's name produces a mean frown
The elders' vote and excommunicate
This braggadocio given the gate

Our Mr. B not wanted in this place
The angry mob now gives him chase
His words produced a flood of gluttony
His infectious voice has been most rottenly

Too much, too often, transparent for all to see
It was either he or audience had to flee
Better to be calm, collected, share a quiet serious word
Or simply listen, be respected and most often not be
heard

∼ ∼ ∼

I'd rather be right
But if I erred
I'd be human

Incorrigible

Scratch me off
Erase me
Obliterate me
No name, no fame
No money, no honey
Outcast - homeless
A wandering zero

I am egotist
Don't believe the above!
It's not so!
I must have been some special something!
All your fault you indifferent society
Am I still alive?
Vibrant? Moving-
More than a ragged corpse
More than a morbid shadow
Damn right I am!

I am ME
The imaginary shelter gives me new clothes
A haircut, resurgence,
Recuperating from some unknown stupor
Shadow yes, even at night
The shelter yes, more
Incorrigible, maybe not!
dissipate, disappear, reincarnate

O.K. I will follow
Twelve step slogan!
There is new lifeblood in this frame
Motion, visible – watch out!
It's my turn to re-enter the world
For all you know
I may be sitting in the theater next to you!

Fictitious Report

Fictitious, false report
 Rumbles of economic downturn
  Another brilliant human is cloned
   The tropical forests in Brazil are on fire!
    Discontent cells everywhere, danger of civil war, race wars
Genocide, holocausts - still too little help, too late
 Rivers becoming acidic - careful, do not drink tap water!
  Pollution, poisonous atmosphere - ominous clouds
   Mask day to day
    Ozone layer penetration now at both North and South poles
Global temperatures rise - Global Warming
 Famine, floods, parched soil - changing phenomena
  Regions near the North Pole melting faster - ocean level rising
   Chunks of icebergs floating south in summer
   Cruise ships beware!

Fictitious report!

Not in my lifetime, you say
 Maybe in yours! Good luck!
  Our world, the most modern, is fraught with danger
  Atomic weapons in the wrong hands?
   Species disappearing "So what?" you glibly declaim.

They measured the ocean level this morning
 It is rising from the melting of both poles
  Some have already paid for a rocket escape to other planet
   Headed toward the moon.

Fictitious report! Fictitious report

≈ ≈ ≈

The word sane
With prefix in
Is questionable, but easy to prove.

chapter fourteen: love and infatuation

The Magic is Us

Engrossed in thoughts of you
Your hazel eyes, your smile
Your luscious red lips,
Your shapely enticing bosom
Statuesque, elegance
All magnets visual
Your quick and witty intellect
Shoot richly in my brain
Love rays consume
And drum up more want
Ah, envious, most accomplished thoughts
So engrossed
An uncanny desire
I wipe out,
Forget the world
It can wait
For now the magic is us

Watch It Grow

If love suddenly lands in your lap
 Cuddle it
  Cater to it
   Cajole it
    Watch it   grow

~ ~ ~

If you can stay in love blind and tense
Go measure your pulse heart and
Take a cold shower or two
Only to find yourself enamored all over again

Love the Greatest

Love. Those four precious letters can spell a period of euphoria and bliss, heartbreak, deep committed involvement and sheer luck, if reciprocated by the person you love. "I love you," spoken with deep sincerity is so special. It is a mystic phenomenon that says "you are my dearest, my closest, my most precious, my partner and best friend". "I love you" means that you express a spiritual bond extending yourself to that wonderful creature that you long for, want to be with, want to share and care for heartily.

Most remarkable are the phases of love with a longtime partner. At first the physical attraction, comes the ever-growing friendship, the building of the nest, the sharing of tragedy and misery as well of feast and fun, each partner giving time and effort to the other. Through many minor and major crisis the love and friendship is tested.

So a wise word to the young person. It's OK to call it love, though it may be simply infatuation, momentary attraction spirited on by the chemicals in our body. Remember love is different, precious, part of the learning curve of life, a lifelong adventure. Love is powerful and all-consuming. It is a compromise, unparalleled, a gift instilled to cheer our hearts.

Piedmont, CA 4th July Parade, 2012

LOVE LOST (but not for long)

Love lost, sore wound pains my heart
So agonizing tender, not easy to discard
But love's chemicals do languish not for long
New strings and chords on love's siren song
Emotion stimulated at first searching sight
Delirious, most delicious dreams all through the night

Two humans search, engage in dialogue
One talks, one listens to the monologue
One overwhelmed with kisses and with gifts
Most enamored from the pedestal he lifts
So interesting, intimate, is set on fire
Subconscious, suddenly a spirited desire

Grotesquely, gingerly, and tenderly
Experiment their love in privacy
The lovers entwined in intimacy bewitched
Transfer of feelings, fondly switched
They so consumed into their own
A tense world beckons as they are alone

For even a wounded, winged bird can heal
The mystery of future life reveal
The humility and gratitude extend
The hope to love eachother to the bitter end
Yet nature in its parables plays many parts
Sometimes the queen of spades or king of hearts

After the first act of love
Followed by more meaningful second
Reassess – bless
Deep emotion and care
If that special chemistry is there
Otherwise – feeling may slip
Downhill in a brainless ship
Let love and passion be on the march
But first give time for battery to recharge

Infatuation

Go, creep under my forehead
And nestle your imprint as I go to bed
Under my scalp the magic tantalizing buzz
Make thoughts irrational, full of fuzz

Curvaceous, beauty, slender
Most exquisite, so tender
A tantalizing, wicked smile
Moves like a gazelle, so please, do stay a while

My testosterone now jumps in celebration
Within me magic joy and much elation
And so you nestle in my thoughts; an apparition
Between what's right and wrong confused division

I retrieve your awesome imprint and your beauty
Like a computer wants to resolve and keep the booty
Your voice a melody - of many tunes
Soothing, cooling, soft reflection shadows of the moons

With compliments and approbation
But more - an energy in syncopation
Electric unspoken feel this close connection
Wonderful, elated now my inner satisfaction

Of belonging, of attraction and of sharing
Approval, great desire, and of caring
Yet am I so infatuated and most blind
Never understood what you in me would find?

Romantic thought
Indescribable bubble over
Thrash, pulsate my heart
I can hardly wait

Women are fickle, foolish, furtive and fantastic. That is not why we love them – it's the chemicals, you know?

ESCORT

Best smooth light linen blue slacks
A golden belt, so shiny
Starry bright blue eyes
A killing smile, goose bumbs collide
Protrudes, toys, teases
A touch of joy
Intuitive electric attractive magic

> Off with my date
> Beef, marinated saucy scallops
> Rice, prawns
> And theatre galore
> Curtains rise
> My hormones bubble
> More touch of the hand so silk-like tender
> Peak, consume her ravishing beauty
> Lucky me! Lucky us!

> Escort of the evening
> A total meal to behold
> And then some!

 ~ ~ ~

Some of us are so brittle we are kept together by pins and paperclips
Until someone staples us together

Her Coy Demands Too Much

Though she's a beauty, anything but tame
A bit airy, stuck up, should I dump her just the same?
So many schemes and materials demands
Seem to dominate her present plans
To ridicule, make me a fool
She does it wily, use her most charming magic tool
To her magic potion I succumb
Her charm and beauty makes me numb
She's so attractive, leaving awful hard
How to convince myself it's time to part?
Her penetrating poise and posture mesmerizes
Her charm and compliments beguile, are full of surprises
She gloats delirious that I am her catch
She feels we fit, not realizing we do not match
Must separate, before it's too late
Or be reincarnated bound by an impossible fate
Too late, her personality soon overpowers
Like crushed pea under shoe cowers
In light of beauty I declare defeat
To part peaceful not be neat
But after love potions leave what is left
I, so empty, lost and so bereft
Let me dance and hold you close once more
For beauty in possession I adore

Living Memorial Sculpture Garden,
Weed, Northern California

I Chased a Sunbeam

Bent down, an awkward omen clutched
Rich treasure looms by navigating nature touched
Like a genie's bottle mystic vision
In awe, I look as if in fog enveloped beauty indecision
"But, I am here," I yell so loud
"Can you see me?" I ask, now proud

Dense fog not yet has lifted
Through many visual image layers sifted
In awesome shapes and sizes
The lovely apparition fled, left impressionable surprises

"Why," I shout aloud, "Can you not hear?
Don't leave, please wait, don't disappear!"
Desperately caught like a fish on a hook
A scary chapter out of my mystery book
Abandoned now, I feel pierced through my heart
The one I wanted and I, a world apart

I feel, I sense, I know you're there
I know you love me with much care
But sunbeams danced and pranced and chased
You gorgeous, marvelous, magic figure now erased
And as in seriousness search, investigate
An optimist, yet I know my fate

Somewhere, someplace I'll see you once again
Rekindle feelings, memories reluctant in pain
Your apparition just to see
And wonder what loving couple we could be

Let it all hang out

Share warm, feeling words
When we eye each other
A sparkle, give of ourselves
Orders, thoughts, renditions
Love, affection recharged
Friendship, closer bond

Feeling restored, re-enforced
New friends come aboard
All intrinsically absorbed
By brain, by unexplained deep feelings
So jovial, pleasant magic story
The metaphor is mixed

Yet an interchange of minds
True friendship does not budge
Do not judge - compassionate emphasis - listen
As I painfully empty my mind
Share deep secrets, feelings
Excitement of the moment

A spiritual, uplifting gift from within
Persuade, awake new thought process
My way - your way
Better - OUR WAY
Eighty, twenty percent, whose side?
Win – win with both heart and mind

≈ ≈ ≈

The powerful feeling of love can sail you into heaven or
painfully torture you in hell
Or both...

Take A Chance

Never too late for a dance or fling
For joviality and time to sing
A merry drink or two
Of course with my dear baby, only with you!

It is the intense moment
Overwhelmed by desire
World cast aside, bold intent
Brings closeness, emotions on fire

Inviting telegraphed glance
Mind blowing posture to attract
It's me. Please me as one of your fans
Desirous, heavenly love bugs now stacked?

So dearest gem, drop all objections
Engage me in my introspection
And join me in this merry dance
Let our love and endearment take a chance

We glide as a pair
across the parquet floor
We whisk and twirl, eternal smile
The melody, your beauty, I adore
This moment! Who could ask for more?

≈ ≈ ≈

I come with love to kiss you
For I miss you
Receptive as we do embrace
Cherish this moment
Time and place

OBSTINATE

Treasure
Baiting - waiting
Waiting - baiting
Frustrations

She - slow, slow - munches last bite
I waited long - was her delight
And with deliberate coy
Lets me wait, plays me as a toy

So self-centered
Never entered
That active me
Buzz like a bee

Instead, slow motion into her own
My impatience - soon an artery is blown
Dare I say: please hurry?
Torrent of accusation: Don't worry!

That's true
She'll say: Don't tell me what to do.
Yet, she loves me
Whatever kind of love that can be

I impart such pleasure
A twosome hand-in-hand at leisure
Some call a spade a spade
I tolerate

And end up with a sexy kissing date

≋ ≋ ≋

Expressing love is a human character
Do it often
But please not on the kitchen table

chapter fifteen: the child

A Little One

Young lads and lasses
Erotic, make their passes
Latch, catch and make a match
Until, nine months later
A little one does hatch

Please don't unload on ma or grandma
Long ago you were their star
Much confrontation and much mirth
Your action that planned this unforeseen birth

One reason why world population rises
Hundreds of babies daily are surprises
Some call it natural conception, some say sex
Happens daily, but overcrowding is more complex

We all have bad habits
And it's all our parents' fault

Children and Offspring

Born helpless, cuddled and cajoled, innocent, yet all too soon not so inno-cent. That is, was, me and you! The toddler exploring, experimenting, toys into mouth, hands holding, trying new foods. Momentarily our tiny bodies wobbling unsteady, we had to be restrained, protected, nurtured. Always with an urgent Yes or No to guide us. You, I, we all were such free spirited children, giggling, laughing, and often in temporary tears, we engaged in everyday life.
Yes, I loved my son Jeff and my diminutive, active, precocious daughter Judy, both inquisitive, ambitious, and full of curiosity with that touch of stub

bornness so common not to follow directions or reprimands. Thank god both of my children became avid readers. We sweated out the routine of nursery school, kindergarten, with groups with other children, always keeping active. There was always momentary concern, deep love. I, coming from the old world, was a bit stricter, yet the message penetrated despite some cries. It was hard love indeed (you know what I mean!).

Lillian, my wife, had the psychological knack to discipline, compliment and encourage them with intelligence early enough that they gained her respect. They did not dare do the testy stuff as eight or ten year olds do, behind one's back. Obviously, we were usually one step ahead of them. Soon caught, reprimanded and lectured to (this was in the 1960's). Don't we parents mostly know full well what goes on in our kids' lives? Yet, to our consternation, it is often not easy to explain and get our child back on the right track when they waver.

Rituals, such as our holidays, prayers, and the simple concept of saying "thank you", (I mean a meaningful "thank you") was instilled into both our youngsters. They were both competitive and good students with good physical balance, and a love of art and music. They shared with close friends and we went on family picnics close to nature. They learned to tolerate rats, mice, lizards, garden snakes, all of which we had in glass cages in our garage to feed and to observe at some point or another. Most of all we enjoyed the frequent visits to the library. We bought dozens of books at yard sales and the flea market. Personally, I accumulated over 1,500 books for immediate reference and reading long before Google. There were also the continental trips to Toronto by car for several weeks, sleeping out in tents or cheap motels.

We also instilled the basic ten commandments in our children, the total mores of our community such as respect for person and country, the importance of telling the truth for you would get caught lying soon enough and that truth matters more than anything. They were taught the importance of sharing and donating, particularly to the poor on holidays, tolerance and respect for other points of view and religions. The latter was easy since I was a holocaust victim myself, lost my childhood, and suffered a traumatic emotional time growing up as a foster child, spending part of my youth separated from my Mother and Father. I became self-sufficient. This work ethic and possible insecurity was passed onto my young kids who stayed out of physical fights except with each other, even though Jeff was four years older than Judy. The key was a deep bond of love and trust. A life-long gift.

Do My Thing – A Plea

No more chains, restrictions – please!
Let me do MY thing now!
I had a tough beginning!
I'm thankful
Amaze you and amaze me,
So many fantastic possibilities,
Tools, teaching, tenacity,
Opportunity and sacrifice,
Drama ahead,
A little comedy too,
Some tragedy,
A work in progress
So please – let me do MY THING!
My thing!
It may be my undoing –

But it's mine!

On His Behind

Ornery and only four
After a warning smack on his behind
He took advantage to settle the score
An indolent, whining, testing brat
So young and sharp and most unkind
Still, after a little spat
Made an angelic boy out of him instead

≈ ≈ ≈

Over-protective mothers
Create neurotic children
Who grow up, raise dysfunctional families
and keep psychologists busy

Camouflage or Soon I will be born

Much of my life is camouflage
In a secret — isolated cocoon
Deep contemplation, self-deluding?
Protected by a fluid of silence

Some old treasure too painful to share
Too scared, ashamed to reveal
Like a liar boxed in his own lie
Too uncertain, lest I be exposed

Please respect me for what I am
Soon I will be born
Share your feelings
Share your passion and pain

Laugh, cry, wonder
Until my first cry
Wait for my time
It will soon come

≈ ≈ ≈

Computers can beat us in chess,
do faster calculations.
Give answers to mundane questions.
But they can't have babies

Birth

They say I jumped out
Of someone's vagina
We all did - pressed, pushed
A struggle, a cry, a caress
The suckle of sweet mother's milk
You too
Our human ritual
Puking, peeing, google-eyed
Utterly helpless and innocent
So we, the bastards and bastardettes
On all sides of the globe
Mature, arrogant, erect
Proclaim our way -
Our value system to be emulated
Horse-shit - if I may say so
Some code before Moses, before
Christ and Mohammed, proclaimed
The power and dignity of man.

A NEW BIRTH

Today a significant date
Morning after; just first-rate
For mother gave in birth pain born
A curly daughter of the mooning morn

Nursed her,
Rehearsed her,
With love and caring,
Hope, happiness and sharing

The babe a treasure of her life so fair
Strong vocal cords greet the new air
So innocent, so pure with charm
Cuddling, cooing in her mother's arm

As if an angel kissed her
This dynamic baby of a sister
In innocence, develop into her own
A sheltered stripling not yet ready to be alone

Seed doesn't fall so far from tree
Babies life not by decree
Blessed with opportunity galore
That's what the Founding Fathers wrote for

So vibrant, talented and skilled
Bring this daughter to be heaven filled

Things change and are lost in translation,
That is why my grandchildren
Don't seem to understand me
Nor do I comprehend their
Modern language and ways

But I love them anyhow

Might As Well Be Me

I am so old, wild, wooly haired
Even the gravediggers despaired
Little kids see me on the street
Run swiftly, lifting up their tiny feet

Stop! Stop! I am OK!
Can't you see the light of day?
I won't hurt you, don't be scared
My face and hair will soon be much repaired

Still I'll never be like you
Ache with pain and feel so blue
Maybe a visitor from planet X
Or even king, they call me Rex

Not my fault visually misshapen
Torture of someone who is agen
But beauty, below the skin
There I am, just one of your kin

Same goal to be content
In the multitude I want to blend
But I am stuck
No such luck
So you see I might as well just be me

Arthur Weil,
his son and
grandson

Stages of Life

The babe's head purple, struggling
Flesh torn born
Into a challenging world
Each stage in life
The heavens and the earth unfurled

Why curious, conscious
Brief innocence helpless
Yet sensitivity, observe – react

Defensive   excessive   cautious
Always learning   absorbing   questioning
Mating   binding   nurturing   family and friends
Growing   knowing
Optimism   realism   new directions

Extroversion and introspection
You wonderful, wonderful world

It is through knowing pain that joy enthralls
It is failure that brings hope, driving force
Out of the mean, new values, our goodness and success
It is through silent, lowly prayers
Infallible or rational belief, in spirit's awe

So blessed
So pure and innocent at first
Tamed. Yes, No, Don't.
Stop
The baby grows, matures
Watch out!
Excited for life's tour

∿ ∿ ∿

*We often know where we go wrong but would still do it
again – there must be a "stupid" gene in all of us.*

If you think your parents were perfect,
then you too must be perfect,
and it's all a happy illusion

Reflections of Childhood

Open a sliver of your secret mind
The unconscious will spill out and over
In waves; your loves and hates
Irrational, but real, will flood
Your valley of present thought
Truth and fabrication intermingle
With the story of your childhood
Your first love
Your mischievous actions
Your fears and forebodings
Morning memories your treasure trove
Intimate, so close to the heart
Almost visual, and sensitive
Relive the best, the pain
See all
Or perhaps it's time
To close the mind's door
Until tomorrow

~ ~ ~

A foot is a foot is a foot
But a kick in the ass
Will have you go a long way.

A Lifetime

Sometime between the age of eleven and thirteen
      We wave good-bye to childhood tots and toys
In growth, leave our homes
      Like bird kingdom, soon build our own nest
Some roam continents, oceans
      Man's curiosity and search unending
To space, ocean floors, caves
      And into his own soul
Endless drive when dear ones die
      Replaced by weak, new awkward relationships
Aged in small abode,
      All these collectibles take, sold, and drowned
The remnant, a frayed old man and woman
      Still coherent, waiting for the latest news
In simple room with bed, chair, few necessities
      In time our soul and memory forgotten
Like that of your great grandmother, great grandfather
      And the last good-bye is
Drowned out by a loud, noisy, busy day
      Graveyards become housing projects

Too soon, Too soon!

Good-bye, good bye.

*How high is high?
That all depends on
your perspective.*

*Two of the author's
grandsons, 2012*

chapter sixteen: ominous storms

Before The Storm

The lightly rippled, placid water
 Becalmed icy melt
  A sequoia tree trunk
  Absolute silence
   Isolated at midnight
    Forbidden, moving, dark
    Ominous clouds
     Away from civilization
      Slow, relaxed, beating
      Heart content
      White blanket
       Snowshoes at 11,000 feet
        All these spell tranquility earned
        A fleeting, lucky time
         Before the next snowstorm

VENTURE Into Iciness

The bristling icy wind
A chill quick movement
Out of my element
Run away, thick woolen underwear
Ear muffs, cap

Yet still red and frozen cheeks
Crunch the virgin snow
Watch the sparkling icy sidewalk
There is a reluctance

Nose and ear tingle of red
How did I get to this God-forsaken place?
There is an air-conditioned world out there!

Survived the storm

Too many gray foreboding clouds
The storm will surely soon tear us to shreds
Hail, rain, wind and thunder
Forewarned, yet I'm a victim under
Nature in its frenzy to itself amuse
To decimate itself there's no excuse
Rivers rapid rush now overflow
As levies break, the devastation shows
(Lightning hits so many tops)
All at once the generators fail
Added a storm of pelting hail
Yes, Mother Nature is in her element
Guilty perhaps, too late to plead or to repent I do
remember great weather yesterday
Earth's change of punishment without delay
Still anxious we do all survive
Thankful that we're still alive
To love, to build and pray
Lucky to experience joy another day

*Lake Tahoe
area, CA
2011*

Dark Clouds

The sky outside so cool and overcast
In sleepy mode I crawl under my soft sheet so fast
And meditate before the sun will reappear
Wonder when I will meet my treasure dear

So much relaxed lose sight of goal
Feel incomplete and just half whole
Seem to fall asleep and disappear
Wonder what on earth I'm doing here?

It wasn't long ago at bedtime in the past
I, the worrier, slept the last
Just to procreate and raise my kids
When other dark clouds beckon in our midst

Or send the youngsters off to where they'd be safe
Try to break mental chains, no more a slave
Until the danger from afar was no more
Receive them back with open door

And move to other venues for a better life
Where peace and freedom soon supplant all strife
Where buildings, scholarly things are most appreciated
Not this dismal existence to which I'm now fated

Why are there still
evil clouds of war
danger?
Each of us
insecure, protective
as a ranger
When all we want
is to be left alone
and pleased
And nourished to
enjoy our
inner peace

Snow Blanket

Careful, the treacherous, icy snow-covered road
  To Tahoe's casinos is a multiple gamble
   I tell myself: Don't be dazzled, frazzled
    The blizzard, bountiful heaps of the big crunchy white
     Snowplows in caravans barely keep up
      Push mountains of the dirty white stuff to road's shoulder
      As we miraculously move on to the casino
Excitement, will I win or lose?
 Will I ever get there in this god-forsaken storm?
  Where are the state highway crews?
  Don't they watch the weather news?
   Sure, they scrape piled impediments off the highway
   Icy, white, mushy, fresh, blinding
    With giant glistening brushstrokes
Paint the crystal, shiny pure antiseptic landscape
 Into the forest-laden picture postcard of white,
  Heavy snows bend branches, jerkily unload the frizzled snow
  The icy wind soon subsides in contrast to
   The beaming sun's rays, blinding blanket of sparkles
   All I want is to get there - gamble, gamble!
    While all join snowball fights, or make their snowmen
Until the cold from ice and snow penetrates the gloves
 And puts pink color into the almost frozen ears, lips and face
  While underneath the cold, grueling brown earth rests
  And the ever-present gray rock formations
   Topped by a foot or so of the white
   Like chiseled, rounded stone statues
    Old rocks withstand these freezing initiations
Let your footprints sink within
 The dense whiteness crunch and pristine
  A heavenly fresh momentous experience
  Most exhilarating, while your breath
   Like cigar smoke circles upward
    Until dusk when the cold chilly, icy wind reappears
    And all return to the casino, their cabins and their cars

      While the white blanket silently stays behind.

Rain

It's 12:37 A.M. We all prayed for more rain!
Yes, our prayers were answered.
Gusts, sheets of torrential silvery rain
Incessant   loud   thrashing   wet
Continuous, heavy drumming sound
Proud   most defying
Like incessant banging of death row prisoners
Or the thunder of bison herds long ago
Never dying

Everywhere, pools of soggy wet
The rows of water pearls bounce on their target
Like bullets against the tank armor
While receptive brown and withered autumn leaves
Plump, rain soaked from tired wet braches earthward
Deliver the cool liquid with it
Like teaspoon medicine gone wrong
Drip-drop unto the hungry earth
A distant thunder (barely audible) pronounced eerie
Evidence of more to come.
Nature's dance, romance of centuries
Like sun nurturing the openhanded land
Cycles of light rain to showers
Stir uneasy emotion, wonder when will it all stop?
As roof drains rasp, move into ever lower-level places
Gutters, creeks, accept the translucent moving flow
The rivulets into roaring dirty, erratic waves
A torrent monster, unstoppable
Much more than we bargained for!

Umbrella, roof, cover
While downstream rivers exact their toll
Nature's foreboding warning
Soon ebb and flow diminish
Rain, flood, so omnipotent, has its own life
Sending a message
An innocent drop became a turbulent monster
Return to the waiting, sacred goddesses of the sea

First Season Rain

Ease off!
It won't rain till after midnight
Hat brim down – boots
Tight yellow rain gear
The first rain in four months is most damaging
Like a drum roll before an execution
An incessant percussion
As bullets like pearls drop bounce
Oil slicks, cars spin out, crashes
Roof cracks, invading leaks
The blast of torrential season
Whipped wind, ready to cleanse all
Old elements newly engrained, not easily forgotten
Windows weep wet and damp
Some basements cracks fissures of dampness
It's nature's powerful omen
To say "Hallo"
With gust, whip and vitality
Storm chill winds penetrate and cause shivering
Complacent I am fast asleep
High above hovers the storm
Foreboding, powerful
The skies' darkening gloom
Pours forth a trillion droplets
Causes havoc and nourishment
The rain gathers into rivulets
Restores the earth
Washes and rejuvenates
Feeds the yearning roots
Soaks crumpled insect infested dead leaves
It's a wash
It's a cleansing
It's time we replenish the golden, crystal fluid
But please, dear nature
Don't overdo it
And drown me!

The World Is Still Here

Is it only an appetizer?
Or test of torture chamber
As the sole of my foot
Touches the floor, like a clinging magnet
Rooted with gravity

> This earth, this hard crust on which we dwell
> Unassuming, unpretentious
> Gaseous fumes, invisible mortal rays
> Dominate our life as we return to our maker
> Gave us a lifetime of tastes and pleasures

In constant periods of joy and pain
Our time so limited, now all will disappear
Suddenly - the bubble of our globe bursts
Protective giant in transit 25,000 miles in circumference
Reflect the sun - torments of heat

> Floods, water, hurricanes, fires
> Too much, too soon, too expectant
> In the distance we see gargantuan shadows
> Forewarning a sharper change - forests disappear
> A new array of blinding burning lights

Self-serving and deluding helpless

≈ ≈ ≈

Like ocean swells, waves,
so our lives are tossed
until the sea becalms
Ever ready for
another
storm

The Iceberg

The craggy rock of ice
A giant spectacle of nature
So evident, so white, in the glistening sun
Juts out of the white blue water
Beware the two thirds underneath!
Ships stay away!

Massive, heavy Greek sirens beckon
And doom awaits - the sonar beeps
I pray to angels to save me
A wide circular invisible force
Pulls me closer
Closer, in the frigid, ice-cold water

The rock attracts me like a dangerous magnet
Stark - shimmering - in the vast sea
To avoid - to admire - seek
I must turn this ship around
Leave fast
Or else? Homeward bound

Wrapped in angels wings
While the iceberg slowly melts
Ever faster, global warming
Centuries old to spell calamity

All is in a state of flux –
even this revolving thing we call the earth.
Keep your balance!

*There are constant disasters all over the world,
like earthquakes, tornadoes, wars, divorces.
One wonders why most of us can sleep so well?*

It's ok to jump two feet ahead and one back,
like on small ocean waves headed ever forward
just don't drown in the process.

*It isn't fair
And I just don't care
What awful nerve
When life throws you a curve*

You'll survive when times get tough
If you live that long, that is

If you brainstorm enough, kick up dust
Energy and new ideas
The modern engine will revolutionize

Man is nature
and
nature is man
but nature persists
and
outlives us all

To internalize deep anger
Is to simmer and brew
Or burn up into ashes

On the outside looking in
Rather be in and looking out
On second thoughts I changed my mind
Run like hell and leave all behind

Fresh snow at Lake Tahoe

chapter seventeen: dreams and visions

It's OK to dream
but I recommend you don't jump off the edge
– the cement below is swift and solid

≈ ≈ ≈

Bloody Dance Awaiting

Black ink transformed to blood red
 This awesome morning, mind in stupor
  After a restless, fearful, almost sleepless night
   I recall this morning's dream, see myself chased
    Haunted by some mysterious dark slender figure
     Guilty images - reprimanded, accused, in utter silence
      As I bathe in abysmal ignorance:
       "What is all this about?"

I sit up at the side of my bed
 Now stark naked
  Eager to move my silver ballpoint pen - write - write
   Piggyback on this inane dream
   Pen now scribbling at full speed
A black, eerie shadow still in my imagination - follows
As I still run hastily to escape the pursuer
I see the edge of the knife with streaks of fresh red
I am innocent?
Who is this imaginary, dark figured chaser?
Images are barely discernible
          I feel slight remorse, a shiver, fear
All this before breakfast!

Unencumbered, in my element
Still half-awake as I dare let my mind wander
Free flow -
Direct
Introspect
Depend and repent

Scribble, scribble - while most of you are still sleeping
  I take a few deep breaths.
     Control yourself! Be coherent!
I cannot wipe the imaginary rich deep liquid red
                            out of my mind
The thought of this picture evinces pain
When will I heal?
Sorrow! Damn it! I hate this anguished feeling
It's in my gut! I know creativity has no bounds
That imprisoned in my gray cells
There is no end, no limitations,
Imagination or the bloody truth?

The pen continues to leap, chase, dance, prick
 It leaks in its glorious, ever-deeper cherry-red color
Impregnating the sheet of reflecting white paper
      Like an amoeba in the lab
 Do I need antibiotics?
Must wash away the red liquid my passion, obsession
Outside the sun now peaks gloriously over the horizon
 Its beams penetrating the red stained glass windows
As if to illuminate the bloody dance awaiting
      Now a fuzzy apparition
      Could it be co-incidence?

 Finally, I skim the second page of this morning's Post
"Red-soaked, bloody murder victim found!"

Feeling

I am a creature of feeling
Nail me on the wall
See how I bleed
Pain streams downward
From broken hearts
The agony of rejection, injustice

Or take my feelings in a helium balloon
As I merrily float, consume the landscape
The news of green, yellow, dark blue rivulets
Stay up there red balloon!
Elated and joyous to return to mother earth
To share my talent, skill and enthusiasm

Landed, home, in the corner of my study
Seriously, I meditate, I contemplate
As my spirit soars
Euphoric, spontaneous, controlled
So powerful, so eternal
That I feel I can speak to the gods.

To run away from yourself
Leads to celebrating your return

To imply is to beat around the bush
But what if there are no bushes in sight?

At Peace

The magic wand of eye fatigue
Colored spectrum into gray
Blurred focus
Brings all I value into oblivion
The eyelids say, "Close"
The body says, "Recline"
Breathe slowly
Anxiety melts
And the magestic
Queen of Slumber
Rules for a while
So, please don't press me for help
For decisions now

*Piedmont
4th July Parade,
CA
2012*

For commitments or deeds
Nature's way to repair, replace
You know my fatigue will wear out
Reality again will stare at me with both barrels
Should I shoot first?
Or go back to nirvana?
Remain in this post-hypnotic state

At peace?

And Here I Am

I step out of a dream
Into another - serenity - peace within
A blue azure infinite sky above
The breezy warmth
Ignites a curious spirit
My eyes open to witness beauty
The silhouette of perfection
That fantasy, like a dream vision
Everything so right today
An iron curtain protects me from the outside world
But here is an aura of peace
Almost in a narcotic trance
No precipice - flutters free
The mind is free to choose, to dare
To think everything and anything, fearless
Below the dizzy ground is distant and foreboding
But here: My space. My time. My being.
A flight into the chapter of my fantasy book
Long sought after path away from reality
I dare not think of the crags and canyons
Of the earth below and about
While I float in the heavenly clouds with my imagined entourage
As if fastened to magical multi-colored balloons,
I am suspended
I close my eyes and with ease
Waft every which way like a bird
Ready to see all, experience all, partake in all
Or perhaps revel in the joy of this moment
This crazy dreamlike self-created vision
And here I am
Not ready to land yet

Flying Carpet

A snow-white distinct pillow's feather suspended
Floated near my bed; mesmerizing, splendid
Wonder from which tiny bird this precious symbol shed
Can I fly on this miraculous magical feather now instead?

In magic mobile I propelled in some delight
The sphere of earth below reflects the moon at night
Clairvoyant see this world suspended from way up high
Mountain ranges, ice poles, oceans catch my eye

A new perspective of global warming first
The deserts dry as plantations lust in thirst
I, way up high, safe, while the globe still spins
Wonder where and which world I'm really in...

Children go to school, fill classes at the universities
Bulging, growing cities ever active full of busy bees
Below in a box, skyscraper, apartment, house
All seem active and ever in front of TV screen browse

Or wallow at home in self-pity
If not at war they do sit pretty
While I gently float above some more
Still, as an observer keeping score

Each person unique and special while alive
Until the engine fails and now at cemetery's door arrive
Before I land, peace and tolerance is my plea
As my flying carpet deposits me back to reality

～ ～ ～

Be sure some of the stuff in your mind
stays hidden...
Some secrets should be treasured

Do not forsake (Unspoiled)

No rousing rollicking rest
No reason - just tired, fatigued
Don't give a damn about the test
Every languished lazy bone has peaked

That drowsy sandman magic full of fuzz
As if magician mesmerized
Into the never-never land of Oz
The mind alert, the body seems half paralyzed

Cuss, let the world go from cradle unto hell
Be still the haunts of ghosts of innocents' bones
Recoup the inner strength we know so well
Know life is flexible, not set in stones

I, eyes closed, huddled, I will recover
Ideas explode in mushroom form
Curled in my Nirvana, dream of my lover
Dare meet the demon and survive the storm

Unspoiled, touched, slightly shaken
The body repairs itself; cells, brain, awaits the call
Goal for success are not forsaken
          Until I wake up...
                    Until I wake and answer all.

Sparks, NV fair

She Pulled Him Below The Wave

He couldn't focus - tempting reactions
Too many worldly distractions
First the high-heeled beauty
Gyrating, tantalizing and haughty
Next invitation, gambling run
Roulette wheel, craps and twenty-one
So clever winning, games are fun
A cabernet or abundant booze

176

Lightheaded he would lose
The losers, lustiness he'd choose
Finally the mermaid beckons
So deep enthralled, he couldn't reckon
As she teased him
Near the waters' rim
Teased, pulled him below the wave
Exciting game, he'd not behave
Gushed salty foam in throat
Choked, deadly, let his body float
Alas his life a chase
Never found in end of tunnel
Life is still in a maze

Rear Door Rustle

12:27 a.m., past midnight, a rustling noise
at the back door, slightly open.
Cool air - did someone tamper?
A faint voice, saying my name, "Art."
I am startled, scared, grasp the consequence
but open the door wider,
look into the barely lit yard.
Full moon. Nothing - silence.
9-1-1.
I wait 4 to 5 minutes, an eternity.
Wait out front. Where is the police car?
Two entrances to my rear home
First police car;
6 foot 4 officer
Second police car
Third officer
Flashlight - nothing.
Why did the door rustle?
I am 30 feet away.
Night, silence, no TV on.
Why "Art"?
It was real, no wine!
I sit alone again
12:55 a.m. and wonder.

Past Midnight

Past midnight
My mind so active and so right
Sharp, acute and so alert
Keen, most perceptive, like a bird

    I question my existence
    Is all life fate and just a chance?
    As young adults do we not choose?
    Wrong step against society, we lose!

I wonder at what height
Our godliness is right
Or as we make mistakes and err
Is God to help or even there?

    And in the early hour
    Why does the sex appeal have so much power?
    At every threshold intervenes and thrives
    A driving force of love directs our lives

And in the AM when the world is still asleep
What foment and ordeal the warlords reap
For on the globe divisions battle bloody war
The killings most distasteful I abhor

    Wonder how to preserve the future of this world
    With global warming, chemicals in air unfurled
    While life spans lengthened with new medical devices
    How can the aged population now maintain in such a crisis?

Or thoughts of writing new ideas
Transcribe my wishes and my fears
Or with the frivolous do pick a bone
Reflect in guilt, next find I do want to atone

A Miracle

A sprightly, beautiful girl
Creeps constantly into my thoughts
While I dress, eat, study,
Am I obsessed?
At silent moments
Wonder what she thinks?
What would she say?
Do I exist?

I see her face, her profile
Her smile, her composition "I miss you!"
The echo of her voice
Cuts through the class
Stifles the noise
Consumes my thoughts
Her silhouette dazzles me

I text
She reciprocates - cheerful
"What did U do today?"
So we do encourage
The buzzing sparks at both ends
Abundant smiles and compliments
Exultation - adoration

A craving for nearness, togetherness
When do we see each other next?
What shall we do together?
Where to eat, where to hang out?
Where to share in silence and closeness?

This new grand feeling
Two sweethearts
A miracle - wrought by heaven
Lived and devoured
A craving for much more!
Please don't tell!

chapter eighteen: humility and morality

Cut the crap

In anger let's *cut through the crap*
Ready to react, to dare and *take the rap*
Seethes and festers, comes to head
Opens sore wound that now must be bled

So, doctrine confused, contentious here directed
No time to think or have our thoughts dissected
The onslaught of attack ends in defense
With malice, venomous vicious shower makes no sense

From brain to tongue a *torrent of words*
Feels like icy dagger twisted deep, *it burns, it hurts*
Perhaps the subject should have been laid to rest
Instead opening a torturous wound of demons all possessed

From thought, to word, to audience intrigue
A dismal, dirty rotten path critique
Do we really need such poison in the air
That makes us cringe and most despair?

Not here, not now,
not never
Turn off the spout
forever

Down to Earth Again

Arrogant, erudite, you ridicule
Hurt, cut, deal most divisive our golden rule
Punitive, painful long to heal
Embarrassed, angry, hurt I feel

Your daring dress, creative color scheme
Not matched, so mishmash as vanilla cream
Extreme mascara, makeup very gross
A few extruding hairs from bottom of your nose

On cue, quick wit, cut your reply
Like acid anger, egg now in my eye
Touch tightly every fiber of my nerve
You over-talk and overact, throws me a curve

In fact, furtive exposition to demean
A touch of demented dictator and fiend
It's time to cringe and compliment
Show some remorse, forge on to a pleasant end

So, if you model modern in extreme
The vision vibrant can be seen
And I your ally, still an able friend
Will dare my duty, you I will defend

Back down to elevation of our earth
Awash with value and self-worth
I want to count you, admire and adjust
So please do not demean, demolish our trust

In you I do admire God-given gift
Your search for scholarly learning gives us a lift
Your level leadership leads beyond measure
So wonderful to see you use such talent, such treasure

Displeasing

Put off the displeasing
Irritating, teasing
Make that phone call
On the contract; stall

Tell your teen-age kids the facts
About life's pitfalls and of sex
Tell a friend you've had it up to here
Share with your partner what you fear

Worry that you spend too much
On the frivolous and such
Level with yourself in later age
Fear you leave world's most exciting stage

Hard to say "I'm sorry"
Disclose true story
Deny when you get a bit sick
Admit that you pulled a trick

Admit all make mistakes
But don't report all your aches
Fear of small place - fight
Only do when the weather's right

Clothes too tight
Or clothes too wide
In critical juncture cannot decide
Dare to do what you feel is right

Dare to laugh out loud
Timid when you're proud
Reluctant to eat the food
Acquiesce when you're not in the mood

So dear one, hate to say good-bye
Hold tears in when you want to cry
Dare to admit that life is good
Critical of your natural look

Scared to say, "I love you"
Deny it if it isn't true
Afraid to cast aside your inhibition
But what if you made the wrong decision?

We are imperfect
Yet stand erect
Sum total of our daily day
We're here to swoon and here to stay

We thrive for truth
And avoid the noose
Your life's a self-created coin
Of many sides with which to join

Our children's laughter we protect
Admire wisdom and use of intellect
After hard day's work we do celebrate
Too busy to worry over some distant fate

For it is now and here
That we sign up with others who are dear
With warm hands we join and clasp
Together, now in unison, to complete our task

∾ ∾ ∾

*In the long run honesty goes further
but a white lie bridges the moment until
your conscience drives you nuts*

*I used to blame my mother,
but then she's been dead for years...*

Well Deserved

So beautiful, attractive
So interested, always active
She is the rave
All the same
She gave
me a bad name
Ruined my reputation
Blabbermouth it seems
Is that why I see
her in my dreams?
How can such an angel
Be my downfall?
I forgave her
Did someone say I am blind?

Piedmont CA, 4th July Parade, 2012

Shall I Shoot Her?

Wrong way, long delay
Exasperated lag, unexpected drag
Can't I get there?
Can't stop, fret there
So I shout out loud, forget my gag

    Complicating, so frustrating
     This game of dating
      The terms unpleasant, to say the least
       Brought her candy, brought her flowers
        My anxiety increased by the minute, by the hours

Will I meet her, will I greet her
Set a seat so close to purr
Hold her right hand, hold her left hand
Will she like me, let me, understand?

    Yes to woo, careful not to overdo!
     Feel like I could shoot her
      She's much cuter
       Touch her hand, touch her finger
       Will she stay and will she linger?
       Vibes correct, how will she react?

Our first session
First impression
Smile and gives me the eye
I reciprocate and almost die
A bit cheery, don't be leery
Tease and please her
Big hug hold her

    "Not there!" like a bear
     As I pine, do entwine
      Right vibration, good sensation
      Getting late!
       What a date! Will it last?
       Has it passed? What a blast.

Your Voice

There is this empty space
Twenty-two hours and 29 minutes
Of silence
Couldn't even take time to call me
Are you angry? What did I do?
Dare I, the other half of the love team
Call you now?
Will you respond with tender words?
Will you exude that feeling of closeness?
Am I not mature?
Why do I feel this emptiness, this void?
This passion and desire?

So there, I hear the phone ring
My heart pounds
Is possession 90 percent?
Or am I a driveling idiot
Like so many of us?
"Yes, this is me."
Your voice is like an angel's back on earth

≀ ≀ ≀

To some, warnings are like bulls' red flag
Ready to attack and face their demise

Grab the Lifeline of Success!

Every day someone you know throws you a lifeline, be it nature's power, a family member, or a close contact or friend.
"You are crazy!" you retort, "My choice, my deed. I am my own person! I don't need help!"

Are we really such creative geniuses to succeed? Are we not molded from childhood by family environment and circumstances? Are our values, work ethic and ego not paramount in what we try to do?

So the lifeline, an open hand, an invitation, provide the first, the second and third job opportunity. Are we poised to venture into our own business or enterprise? Saved money, bank loans, relatives, family, luck are all our lifelines. Even the seeds of an idea, the dedication to study, to plan ahead and execute does not come from just within, but often some person, some inner urge and drive to succeed, sets forth and motivates this positive action.

"It's OK to get help, to get advice! Didn't we go to school for enough years to fill our brains, to learn the skills and tools for our future?"

Aren't the ups and downs of early life, in your twenties and thirties, experiences that fashion thinking? Don't we need to feed our egos constantly to compete, to improved, to move ahead? Free men and women all want to climb the economic and social ladder. A lifeline here and there helps. Even if at times we fall off the cliff, fail temporarily, our human nature dares to try again, somewhat smarter, more prepared. Why not use all the ideas, talents and tools around us and dare put ourselves into the picture?

If you start a business, with help of a CPA, an attorney, an advisor, a banker, well planned – go to it! Whether it is in service, manufacturing or sports, the opportunities are endless. Bring your dream to fruition. It's OK to be a bit fearful, stumble, but make sure you have enough capital, planning and skills plus the work ethic to succeed.

Good Luck!

Hard to Say Good-Bye

You ask and ask and pick my brain
It's late in life, still I'm not insane
And wonder as ideas from brain do spill
Full of desires and strong action by the way of will
Stay happy, healthy, as your goal
Sell your heart but never sell your soul
Order body to exercise and dance
To dare the project, take a chance
To buy and buy man-made junk
Foolish to hide it all in some old attic trunk
Stay happy, healthy, as your goal
Sell your heart, but never sell your soul
Still want to satisfy the palate with morsels that tease
So tasty and tender they must please
The hum of engines still thunder in my head
Browse on, ferocious fill until I am dead
Stay happy, healthy, as your goal
Sell your heart but never sell your soul
A crazy, busy, foolish world
Where values, plans often into the abyss are hurled
And spend or waste much precious time of life
Soon dissipated as if into pieces by a carving knife
Than why do I cherish life each day?
Despite all old age when it creeps in
Run away? Hell no, I'd rather stay
Do what I can, it's not a sin
Stay happy, healthy, as your goal
Sell your heart, but never sell your soul
Most plans carried out or often now abated
What comes and is mostly fated
Comment, we did it all
Stood proud, erect and tall (and did not fall)
Weak knees, bones, hearing, eyes tired
Yet all about is still admired
Too bad, as much as I try, It's simply hard to say "Goodbye."
Stay happy, health, as your goal
Sell your heart, but never sell your soul

King On the Mountain

Success begets success
Until on the peak or mountaintop
I dare defend my spot
An unexpected wind
Brings unpredictable weather
And I reluctantly come down
Knowing I must bend to the elements
Even the king on the mountain
Soon leaves the pinnacle
Grateful to kiss the earth below
And be one of us.

Keep Your Cool

Keep your cool
With all those others
Interlopers
Gropers
Bad decision
Ego-driven
Well meaning
Scheming

Love, leave
What's good for you
What's good for me?
You one
You too
If only they knew
Told you so
Knew it all the time

Be gentle
Be patient
Forgiving
And pray
It shall pass
This day
Who is the fool?
Not he, nor she
Who keeps their cool

How to survive
Stay alive?
Apart
Together

chapter nineteen: flashes of my life

Could I Live My Life Backwards?

Caution, I back the car
Out of a long driveway, not too fast
Slow, exact... Back! Back!
Back in time
Memories?
I wonder: what if I could live
My life backwards?
See each movement, wonder
Should I have known better?
Ashamed, I said such foolish, stupid things
Decide where to take a chance, cross that bridge?
Turn at the fork right instead of left?
Euphoric, get entangled
Only to be disappointed

Err, apologize, and suffer
Portfolio sold, revised, upside down
See more of the world from west to east
Spend what I saved more wisely
Slowly, ever so slowly, meditate
Eat up the fantasy of beauty all about
Better move forward
They tell me the President's not going to the moon
Instead, another war; said would be over very soon (in '05!)
Many casualties, everywhere the enemy does lurk

Yet, I too am busy - life, study, work, study, work
Why do we want to live like kings?
In this material world of collecting things?
Buy the latest computer toys
Live for the moment, hold your poise
Entangled into global warming
Stem cells, universal health
Not yet a slave for riches nor for wealth
My life backward, you say?

You choose your direction every day
It's up to you to work or play
Take time to canvas and to vote
For change and act now on the road
Still quality time for family and friend
The dream of better life should never end
As inevitably it will
Go backwards with knowledge of today
With care for everything I say
Umbrella of my family and friends
Their love and comfort never ends
And as I make my bed with care
Pick the best of past with much to spare
The tastes, the bites
Past moments full of rich delights
A miniscule dot on cosmos scene
Rejoice in new ventures where I'd been
Exhilarated, upbeat, rich, directed
This precious life of mine inspected
In gratitude and full of thanks
Join peaceful ghosts' and angels' ranks
Step back, more back - all life's so brief
For in my heart I do believe!

～ ～ ～

I Would Judge

Addicted to late night TV
I binge to escape from me
Absorbed in visual inane
If I were outside of me
I would judge such a person insane
Or certainly in need of help

191

Flashes of Childhood

Flashes of childhood: licorice, raspberries
Pungent smell of red, ripe apples
Climb the pear tree
Bite into the rich, ripe juiciness
Sugary fluid dancing over my cheek

From there, the grandeur spy in awe
Wide vistas of green-yellow meadow
Nearby, a burbling, crystal clear brook
Glistening like a snake, meandering
Past worn out barns, past dilapidated farmhouses
Lush green, licking the moist riverbank

The song of a mating game
Distinct croak of frogs
We'd catch and release them
Through bushes
Pushing away spider webs
Stop – stop – listen

See the slithering garden snake
And with daring precision
Lightening quick, grab below the head
Hold trophy high
 – A victorious gladiator

The constant buzz of pesky mosquitoes
Swarming unkindly, attack arm and neck
With an angry slap – squash with a tinge of red
The bees buzzing, facet-eyed, spying blooms
Colorful butterflies bobbing, germinating flowers

From pistil to pistil, sucking sweet nectar
We'd catch the helpless winged specimens
Capture in alcohol clouded glass jar
One more trophy, not thinking that all life is brief

I was only eight, 1933, dark dawn ahead
A skinny curious innocent lad
In Hanover, Germany, on the advent of Hitler's rise
My life one of decade's peaks and depressions
Ribald, roving, proactive, adventurous nature
Colors and nature roil and rattle from my toes to gray cells
A constant craving gift even now as I am eighty-seven

Or lengthwise, roll down the hill
Tease, push, and wrestle
Pinch each other, as little boys do
Or catching the brown, beetle-like May bugs
Antlers on their male counterparts
Trap in spacious cigar box
Fill with green leaves
Abundant meal for the innocent insect

The rustle of windblown leaves
Brown and yellow mountains
Half decomposed in the sun's rays
Dancing oblivious
Watching the sunbeam dance to
The cantata of chirping birds
Answering the mating call
With innocent chirps
Painting the landscape with
Nature's music

Stepping between cow dung
Cows chewing, clinking cowbells
While the morning crow of the rooster
Announcing the dawn
Soothes the hens, jostles
Pink pigs in their messy pigsty

Competitive, I jumped from the roof of the barn shed
Into hay bales spread
Like a yellow mattress, oozing fresh cut smell

Dry grass for the winter store
Jumped again – my right hand
twisted
Fractured in two places
Utterly painful, my tears and
anguish
Mixed with pride

The surprise of sudden rain
Often ignoring shelter
Soaked to the skin
All wet and natural
This time of bliss and innocence
The laughter of those moments
Embellished in my being
How lucky to remember
Reflect – 70 years later
With barely a scratch

*Arthur as a young boy on holiday. He is
the thrid face down on the right side of
the doorway*

I must have loved the world
As even today I can fly and fall,
Lift my bent, older, body erect
Smile content, excited with living
Not yet ready to define my memories
But ready for tomorrow
Tired eyes, refreshed

Face the Real World

Furtively, quickly
My mind tick tacks, frolics
With vignettes of yesterday
Infatuations, love encounters
After the duty list of morning
I search for time
Private time, loving time
Space, protected in a cocoon
With you
If only for a moment

To be complete
To feel my body
Communicate with your spirit
And like electric waves
Surging within me
Reach out
To the unreachable
Until it is time
To hatch, crawl out, away from you
To live I must face the real world.

Picture Book

Visual — moving album
Picture book
The images of my life
Family — friends
Photos of yesterday
Still very meaningful!
The baby, first steps
On dad's lap
Birthdays with friends
Chuckles and tears
Memory recalled
All still there alive
So real
They even whisper
Some seem to move
I embellish
Yet so many gone
While I still love
And reminisce
I close the picture book!
Will my grandchildren absorb?
My wonderful collection
Will all these images
Be lost — discarded?
Better transfer to a CD

It's Okay To Cry Sometimes

Sometimes, not very often
I cry pearly, salty tears
But not very often
The anguished feeling
The tightening stomach
Recollections
Many are dry painful tears
Accompanied by a silent, grueling moan
So I cry

I miss her
I reproach myself for so much I have not done
The reminder of a missed opportunity
The faux pas or embarrassments
The love stripped into oblivion
So many loving opportunities gone by the wayside
She was a beauty, beautiful!
I cry

And then I joyously cry
Beautiful day, our wedding eve
My first-born son
My awe at Yosemite or the art museum
How thankful, how grand
All mine
So I cry, somewhat rejoiced
I cry

As the years wither
I accept my place in the world
What is – is
I cry at eulogies for friends
This time wet salty tears down my cheek
Love, memories, feelings,
I cry
It's okay – It's okay to cry sometimes!

Party Time Birthday

Time Out: Party-Time, Self-imposed!
Why not?
Time to celebrate
Excite the spirits ever so often
Nourish my soul
Not a hedonistic dance
Taste buds sharp
Rich, ripe colorful odor
Of peaches, nuts, wine
The zesty fruity smell
From liquor, the dress-up
Dress down, my party in latest fashion
Gather my friends; My birthday!
Cooked beef
Swiss imported cheeses
Blueberries and raspberries
Boysenberries
Fresh lox on fragrant warm bagels
Sherbet, ice-cream of many flavors
A special time of remembrance
And laudatory speeches
Drama ending in comedy
Stories and vignettes
Entertainment, music
Magicians, cards, gifts
Riotous poems
Slideshows and artwork
Lyrical songs, violin, piano music
Surely it could be arranged?
Forget about the outside world
There'll be plenty of time
For war, recession, disease
Not now! Not today!
A void filled by me!
My own barrel of fun birthday party
Any time I desire
At a moment's notice

Values

My mother gave me values
Honesty, respect, diligence
But the other 99% I have
To learn everyday the hard way

The Eyes in Younger Days

I wonder about the color of my eyebrows
Once brown, long lashed,
Now the silvery intrusion -
Reflects my age
Blood vessels feed my dark-brown hair roots
The body's chemical compounds
Strands dark brown or silver
Is it just my eye brows, my eye lids?
My time will come
My time has come

I stare deliberately in a daze
At the half-moon hidden behind gray clouds
Or see perhaps a figure of a slender beauty - I know her
People hustling home
Some angry, some of feline kind, in small parts of conversation

My eyebrows protect my link in a chain of people
Father, Grandfather, Great-grandfather, Daughter
Mind and eyes now - sharp I am wide awake
I see each object clear precise like the lens in a camera
I register and capture in a vast memory bank
Eyelids blink and eyes focus
Rests upon my stable strong face
The sculpture in the garden
The eyes and brain cells alert
Who is it?
Of course, that's me in younger days.

Digital Family Photos

Digital Photos;
Distinct electronic reproduction
Shades, shadows, visually enhanced
The featured colorful romance

The mammoth, magnificent
Memory stick
Active, past now; a fantastic flick
While nature's blooming white petals so profuse
Illicit love now just old news

Art and Ilse

Arthur as a boy with Aunt Ilse

Art's Grandaughter

Dare we ignore the camera's eye
A new house-warming spy
Events like young and posing cuties
To special wedding album beauties

A feast, a house, a concert pianist
A birthday party, lovers kissed
Pictures of a singular capsule of time
So many healthy, robust and in their prime

Some pictures faded and pitted
The scary truth barely admitted
Many faces blessed no more
Some now dead or distant, yet we still adore

All stored, filed, etched, engraved
Do we really want to see how we behaved?
Yet all such very vivid memories
I, the eternal photographer

Only a reflection in a glass case

I hate to clean up
Especially my own mess
But there comes a time
When I face my own maturity

chapter twenty: fantasy of youth

There is a fine line between imagination and reality. Which comes first? It creeps up, childlike; the little girl, the princess, the macho boy, the warrior, the policeman, the spaceman, Superman. Thus we grow into adolescence, half-baked, hormones raging. We emulate movie stars, superstars, collect the latest gadgets and fads, we become addicted to computer games. Somewhere between the ages of 11 and 13, as imaginary adults, we partake in the circuit of our community. Luckily there is still skating, ball games, adolescent fun, and the inevitable resentment against authority. We study at school because we have to. We bond with special friends.

Ahead is still the uncertain future.

Often no one dares talk of a war to come, of public duty or the military, or the burden of raising a kid long before a parent's education is completed. All we know is there is a vaguely guided, roughly planned tomorrow, along with duties, obligations, and "must get up in the morning". Birthdays, holidays, vacations, are the happy unifiers and interludes. Grandparents, older relatives and friends die. Life goes on at a fast pace. Torn between play and obligation, as a youth, it's not yet our burden or choice.

Yes, in those early uncertain teen years emotion and exploration run rampant. We are between being youngsters and young adults. In older times children had to grow up much sooner and were adults at a much younger age. How lucky we are today, with all the love, nurturing, learning and exploring ahead, and the world at our fingertips for the rest of our lives...

Too soon our time will come!

Get a trainer, life sustainer

No brainer
Get a trainer
Life sustainer

Diet Riot Fly it
Stretch
Wrench
Quench

It's often a long day in
a short life
You have to suffer to
appreciate it

Exercise
Try on for size
Muscles tender - surprise

Once well rounded
Pummeled and pounded
Hundred per cent all out astounded

Love, friend
May it never end
Partnership penned

Promises, personal training pal
Gave a heavy sell
Worthwhile
You know full well

Piedmont CA 4th July Parade, 2012

Art's Granddaughter, 2012

Imprint of Life

Comfort the son
        See the father
                Touch the mother
Honest, sincere
Imprint of life

No replica, no mirror
Just snippets,   embodied
Ingrained, digested
Instinctive personality
Regurgitate

      and in innocence

              passes on

Osmosis

    Inheritance

        Way of life

In Our Tempting Youth

In tempting youth we dare
Investigate; tease the lion's lair
And if his paws do mangle,
Bruise
Gamble that our heads we may lose

It's ours to taste and test it all
Invincible; get up after each fall
So much to see, to smell, experiment
Young revolt, we do not bend

Vibrant, vocal, easy to reject advice
Speak our minds as we arise
We're dreamers, schemers, not yet burned
Not yet mature, our oats not earned

To Be Twenty-Five Again

I wish I were twenty-five again
I'd hold the umbrella and stop the rain
And shelter you and hold you close
And kiss your lips and the tip of your nose

I would whisk you off to shores unheard
To pinnacles and jungles, see the prettiest bird
Share the native culture of the season
And squeeze and kiss you without reason

Empty my heart and feelings deep
Share the secrets we must keep
So true and loyal as the whitest dove
Proclaims the closeness of our love

Perspective

Show me the pictures
Impressions deep
Focus and perspective
Right angles, shades
Christ, Moses, Buddha
Or cumulus clouds licking the sky
The two-year-old twirling toddler
The worn face of a purple-hatted old lady
The smashed car
In front of the RR engine
An extinguished birthday cake
Show me the picture
Of myself
In front of the mirror
As the years travel
So quickly
Asking
"Is it really me?"

Fantasy of Youth

Reluctantly I prostrate myself
Bathed in a shower of guilt
I ask for forgiveness

Absolution – yet this overpowering sexual urge
I can't erase, can't purge!
I fight on like blind warrior
Yet what have I done precisely?

Why can't I curb my desire?
Chemicals in the bloodstream set my brain on fire,
Victorious illusions in each vein
Rejuvenation bordering on the insane

Mind joyously fantasizes sex
Power, dominance, these desires most complex
Goals thwarted, what a mess
Conquer dreams for my success

Squash my detractors,
Get even, hedonistic hexes dance
Occupy every stage in my brain

Forgive – forgive,
What does this mean?
A dancing devil called urges
Emanates all over the body

Stay distant before it engorges you
Am I some mutation?
Or just feeling a rebirth of youth
Eager to love, not to harm
The chemical thwart mind and thought

Yet the love cloud embraces,
And forever chases
Elevates my spirit
Never sated

Half-Baked Adult

I hold the your tiny hand close
Hopscotch jump, next to me
I escort you, grandchild, into new worlds
Parlors, palaces of heavens
With magic rainbow colors
Of blue, purple, red, yellow
Away from busy mankind
Your small soft grip a comfort

Peaceful, serene, welcome
We fly in the stratosphere
Away from its crust, high over our Earth
With destructive, magnetic force
Away from urban centers
Glide higher above
Below the masses roam
Gleaming, straight 100 story
Skyscrapers filled with busy ants
Called people
And jet planes zoom like big bugs
Land their passengers like flies
Buzzing about – each destined with purpose

You are so fresh, pure, and clean
So innocent
Come, let us jump into our magic kingdom
Of toys, of animals, from paradise
With eager open eyes peruse
The magic
The torrent river – now becalmed
Crystal blue, with tropical fish
Begging to swim in
Let us go into this fashionable
Building, speedy elevator to our apartment with ultra-modern
Kitchen to concoct the tastiest stew

Scrumptious salad
A fruit bowl of berries
Blueberries, blackberries, raspberries, strawberries
With a colorful dish of yogurt
And ice cream of every flavor
To boot

Let our tantalizing taste buds roam
And we revert to the joy of childhood
Yes, yes, everyone we meet
Greets us joyously, hello
How are you?
Wonderful day!
Don't the flowers smell magnificent?
It's our separate peaceful
Tranquil world

But child, it is the safe, fenced garden
In which to roam and play
Computers, banks, toys, small Disneyland
Puppets and fairies to project you
Clowns to amuse you
Animals like dogs, cats, horses for tricks
Your own miniature transportation

Child – let your imagination roam
Dream of your wants, play to your heart's desire
Eat wisely, play and play some more
But when the hour strikes twelve
When your 12th birthday comes
You must leave
The hour of life's division strikes!
No more to return to that other world!

Mature, consequences
Responsibility – accountability
NO MORE A CHILD!

Captain of Your Destiny

The sperm and egg unite
The chromosomes and genes just right
The miracle of growth inside
To light of day born just so right

You are that special creature
Every dimple, smile and feature
Passed on for centuries at each station
By ancestral prolific regeneration

If you succeed or maybe mess up
Change, do well or even stop
A hearty smile is a worthy communication
And the reward to reach honor, elevated station

If you fall short, not nature's fault
Get up, wake up, for opportunity called
The free world's open, it's your choice
It's now your doing and your voice

Change for the better
Be a doer, be a getter
Won't cost a farthing nor a cent
You are the director, do you understand?

So many promises from childhood 'til now
So much taming, learning to wipe your brow
On this vast ocean you are master of your fate
Steer to a happy future, before it is too late

≈ ≈ ≈

To be dishonest is to go out of your way
With burdensome lies and excuses, until you get caught
And have to pay the price

You know the end will come
So on your way, make of life the best
Nature soon will take care of the rest

I could swoon
To the tune
Like a loon
But the shrill
Of his bill
Can kill

Stay away from troublesome people
They may be contagious

chapter twenty-one: crime and punishment

Execution

The bottom line:
 "Not dead yet!"
  Epitaph almost written
  Still time for life
  Guilty as hell
   Deed done long ago
    Gruesome, bloody, painful
   Exact punishment, now
    Prisoner – powerless to resist
   Condemned
     Confused – his life flashes in front of him
    Still, he proclaims innocence
     To Christ his confessor, the world
     Some believe him
      The evidence shows otherwise
      Had single parent – shunted – abandoned
      Railroaded – innocent, his claim
      Stepped on, caged, despised, abused
      Missed his boat long ago
       Guilty after birth
        All society's fault
        They pray outside the prison gates
        "Preserve his life!"
        Again he shouts – proclaims
        "It wasn't me, I am innocent."
          The haunting ghosts of his victims know better
         The executioner at midnight
         Waiting for last minute reprieve
         The governor declines
          The pastor – priest – Rabbi
          Burst of light
           Coupled with a buzzing alarm clock
            Electrified in sweat, confused mind
           Grueling sound of justice
           Get up – get ready
           Call it punishment!
            I shower, listen to the morning news
            Eat my breakfast, clinking gloom
            Back to work, out the door
            Two worlds apart

Not Easy Come

A flaw, some have to scheme
To con, extract and cream
Clever, educated, dare in stealth to steal
Calamity, escape, soon captive, life unreal

At first, prosperous, uneven tune
Pricked phrases polished, prune
Jolly adventurer masterful music degree
Drowned in a worldly song of the sea

Caught cheating on the first offense
Incarcerated in a cellblock for some recompense
A whiz, a charmer, played his cards
Exacted favors from the guards

Though time in prison tedious
Soon released, confinement hideous
Soon escort to ladies on an ocean cruise
Best job to con and joyfully amuse

Alas the lively wells soon dried
Accused, indicted that he lied
To foreign shore our lady's man
Still received gifts for quite a span

In innocence, preached gift to all
Lengthy sentence in an 8 x 10 stall
Excuse, his dad dishonest; no free ride
Confined regimentation must now abide

Worked in prison chapel, sometime prayed
His dream of super wealth dismayed
Missed wife, missed freedom's choice
Denied, now simply a long-term prisoner, one of the boys

Falsehood

Did you know him?
Thus murmurs falsehood, untruths passed on
Devastating – so unnecessary
Reverberates, reflects upon the characters
Eats into flesh, beneath the skin
Ignominiously harmed
Scarred by untruths

Of liar covers the innocent victim
Unless squashed early, deep regret
The lie repeated often enough
Becomes the black and deadly truth to many
Like an infested cancer
Multiplies and destroys all contact
Too late to disinfect, to isolate, retract

Expose the villain – too many believers
Walk in devil's shoes, stomping
Only shallow shadow of the poisoned corpse
Tarnished and mutilated by angry lips
Filled with poison's self-destruct
Be rescued by the angels in their upward flight

≈ ≈ ≈

Frustrations

Baiting - waiting
Waiting - baiting
Frustrations

She - slow, slow - munches last bite
I waited long - to her delight
And with deliberate coy
Lets me wait, plays me as a toy

So self-centered
Never entered
That active me
Buzz like a bee

Instead, slow motion into her own
My impatience - soon an artery is blown
Dare I say: please hurry?
Torrent of accusation: Don't worry!

That's true
She'll say: "Don't tell me what to do."

~ ~ ~

Free Bird

Man censures
Woman corrects
Government restricts
Bombarded by warnings

"Keep Off..."
Always restrictions
Too many
Beaten into mental submission

I think it
I know it
Why can't I say it
The art of convention

I hate it!
Speak, speak
Let me listen, let me listen
I want to be a free bird

The Prisoner Within

Boxed in by choice
the trivial duties of the week
Family, friends escape to sports,
like theater endless emails,
phone with very little time to contemplate;
"Where am I?"
"Where is the inner me?"
"How can I fulfill my secret wishes?"
"Who am I really?"
"What happened to my dreams of yesterday?"

So much to do obligations
So little time
Despite good planning
Honors, politics, earned awards –
all never enough surprises - let down
So much demanded, open handed
Another reception, another request with a "yes"
I will answer, and all I want to do is see the beach
Hibernate, water, the clouds roll by, see them boil

Yet am I so conditionally programmed?
Are will and old ways one?
Are all these routines, security, laughs
Not wholesome, worthwhile human exercises?
Do I have to be a soldier on a distant battlefront?
Fear for my life? The last line of defense is here!
We modify, improve - but total change is rare
If we are relatively comfortable, why change?

Invisible chains disappear
Your inner freedom is now dear
Finance as master of your time
You, the architect, that's no crime
You'll find yourself with gusto and zest
Hard work and miracle you will pass the test.

Wipe Him Out!

I cross his name out
Erased
A gangster's mark
To wipe him out
Waste him,
Kill him
Away
He is my antagonist
Competitor, nemesis
Danger
It's either him
Or me
The blood runs deep
I cross out
His name
That's the dead end.
No remorse

Your laundry list of things for me to do
is meaningful, excessive and 10 years too late

Never More the Devil's Slave

I stiffen at the gory thought
Cadaver to the morgue was brought
Two deadly bullet holes the cause
Angry shooter wouldn't pause
To mob some silly debt not paid
Send him to sweet St. Peter's gate!
His kids now victims, orphans innocent
No justification and no recompense.

Victim in late terrible teens - an addict, user
Stubborn, know-it-all, dealer and abuser
Born and grew up in the hood
Consequences never understood
Wrong crowd, booze, women, stolen goods
Caught, sentenced to juvenile
Stubborn, wise guy now his style.

Tragic, too late
Inevitable fate
Scenario in poverty rehearsed
Unjust society is cursed
The bugs and insects busy in your grave
You are no more the devil's slave
Leave ruin broken hearts behind
The search for peace you'll never find

*Living
Memorial
Sculpture
Garden,
Weed,
Northern
California*

Lost My Cool

With vigor stepped on one stubborn empty carton
To crush, squash for recycling
Like yesterday, when that mosquito
Sucked my arm, interrupted by a lightning squat
A red ooze of my own blood
The mosquito carcass barely recognizable
She had done the biting deed
Where do these rascal irritants come from?

I run into a malaise, tide turns against me
Demeans and ridicules
Ego like a hand grenade ready to explode
My blood curls, froths
The demons in my head dance viciously
And soon this relaxed, even-tempered hulk
Turns into the unwanted monster
With a biting, icy, stinging tongue
That shies and scares even the devil himself
Do I need anger management?
Perhaps

But icy showers, renewed awakenings
Cool head slowly reforms this tyrant's rant
The ugly demeanor, exhausts and plays out
Like the third act of a bloody, deadly drama
And compose, recognize new feelings
Eyeing a beauty, imagining oceans turn timid, calm

Soon regret and forgiveness replace
This illogical rant, banter, irregular display
And tamed nature, my human consciousness
Socially decent behavior transplants
What shortly before was the devil incarnated
I don't want to face myself
It is my Doppelganger, the self against the self
To preserve myself and the human race

The Cart

The old man, gray, whiskered beard
His cart   step by step
Feet touch the sidewalk
The wheels   creak - creak
Out of the corner of his own worn out, tired eye
Alert, the hot, humid air
Spells spare

But here in front, his candle, his belongings
His cart   his all - his all
His plastic bags with dirty blanket
With morsels; half wrapped burger, bottle
Could be water
Or some booze from last night
A small worn pillow and lots and lots
And lots of old plastic bottles, cans and knick-knacks

As he   pushes - pushes
His life's estate
Everything: rags, destiny
His mind on the next step
As the curb narrows

It is his basket that fills the dream
Of a cold beer
The touch of an old lady holding his hand
But he pushes the world away, oblivious
The cart   symbol of our time
Thank you God
He can still slowly walk away
They say he is still alive

〜 〜 〜

We relish the just defeat of our enemies,
cautious that the pendulum does not reverse
when their time comes

We are all prisoners to our own shortcomings
Just doing time

Deviants

Some deviants never let up
Caught, quickly tried, that's the rub
Convicted with harsh sentence
Punishment; sent away, little repentance

"Put them away for good," the mob proclaims
"Cast the vermin off a cliff" their aim
The callous mob vents mortal anger
And in their joy and reveling, a doppelganger

The deviant is caught
All is not for naught
Re-educate! New safety celebration
Re-affirm all in annunciation

They dance, shout, dressed in promiscuous garb
Shrouds and rags or large olive tarp
Walpurgesnacht their daily ritual
Time to tame and tarnish now habitual

Deviants are now incarcerated
The next bunch now still ill fated
Closely watched, demeaned
Institutionalized, isolated and now screened

More and more iron fists rule society
The prisons full, no more propriety
Habitual, mostly not
No effort to rehabilitate their lot

Soon a strict, dictatorial control
Reward the spy and too the mole
Suspicions everywhere with freedom lost
Just as a military camp and downright bossed

It's time for mass and prison break
For freedom's role and heaven's sake
Topple rulers, create vast civil strife
Break chains of prison, fight now for a decent life

chapter twenty-two: sex and all

In our formative years, sex seemed as important as food and exercise and quite as delicious and intense. Once we accept sex as part of human trait and behavior, we safely participate, indulge and that is healthy and good. Unfortunately in some parts of the world many millions of women are still considered "UnterMenschen", sub-human, to be ruled and dominated in law, religion and sex by men. In ancient times a man could have several wives, or concubines. Even today the Moslem religion allows up to four wives. When I talked to a Washington D.C. foreign-born African taxi driver now living in the U.S., he still referred to his many wives "back home" in Africa as a matter of fact. Mormonism (and studies of chimpanzees and Orangutans in the wild) shows how the dominant male monkey protects his harem, just like in many other animal kingdoms. Dr. Arthur Weil, my distant relative (and namesake) after many years of research on white mice in his Northwestern University laboratory, wrote about males and females in many books. He researched and discussed the differences in nature, makeup and chemicals of the male and female brain in the 1930's.

So what? The growing tendency and new acceptance of a percentage of the population pairing up with their own sex and gender, cohabiting and having intercourse, dates back to Greek and farther ancient times. There is also love, camaraderie, partnership and co-dependency, to consider in a relationship, although one or the other is often sexually and one sensually dominant.

It is the physical contact and exhilaration that we often cherish, although some may also have fetishes that even at my old age I frown upon and don't understand, though the fetish in question is hopefully by two adults acting in mutual consent.

Is has always been a necessity, an outlet or just the natural phenomena that many forms of sex and cohabitations are here to stay. Unfortunately, many people in relationships stray to experiment outside their habitual sex lives, often risking their relationships, marriage vows and responsibilities of parenthood.

Sadly my own father was a traveling salesman who had his wily times on the road even after he was married, to the chagrin of my mother. He turned out to be an absentee, indifferent, lousy, non-attentive, unsympathetic and unconcerned father. The thought hurts me to this day.

Do I recommend continual sex regardless if you are even over ninety? Of course I do. I do! Proceed with caution! So you see, dear friend and reader, I love to talk and share and learn about sex, the most advertised phenomena in our world. Can I function without it, as some isolated prisoner who compensates? Of course we all can, but against our will and nature. Love, sex, physical desire, the engagement of flesh against flesh either real or imaginary are here to stay. Be part of it. Be not ashamed. Everything within reason. Your life is short, useful and compassionate. It is the modern age, yours to participate and enjoy.

Overcome With Sex Glands

Stop it!
I told my mind
So constantly overwhelmed by her
Thoughts, feelings,
Inflicted on me
As if all is doped
Foraging in dreamland for her
As if
Two warm-blooded lovers together
When, in truth, we are really far apart
Even when I pray
Her vision appears, she clouds my mind
As I return to full bloom
Flower - lovely gentle
What magic power?
Are our sex glands so powerful?
Overcome all? Dominate?
Ours a world of infatuation, of love
And then there is the real world
"Stop it!" I told my mind

~ ~ ~

Like lovers, we do not need flashlights every day,
But when we do, they are nowhere to be found

Tumbling Down

Censure much
But the prurient, sexual aberration
Mind blowing
Dreams cheat just a bit
Can't be all straight and proper
There is excitement
Prisoner of infatuation
Body over mind
The risk of life
But not on the edge, tumbling down

The Slut

The slut
In the rut
Kept a little mutt
Sold her wares
To any who cares
Took guts
Answers to other sluts
While flesh she bares
Overdose ended all affairs

～ ～ ～

Come To Me Lover

Come to me lover
Beauty of my daring dream
Soothing angelic voice part of our team
Rings of eternal bliss

Come to me lover
Cheeks, neck, ear, gently does engage
Touch of a rhapsody composed by a sage
To tantalize, evoke that magical thrill

Come to me lover
In our arousal with unspeakable delight
Like blinded teen effusively acclaim at first sight
Sensual moment ride on lover's beam

Come to me lover
Our encounter impregnated in memory divine
Ours the moment, yours and mine
Forever ecstatic
Relive this feeling "to the end of time."

Mood to Love

Magic chemistry magnet toward my love
Marvelous majesty of our union
          Elixir of vibes released
          From brain to every human nerve

All plans, duties subjugated
The primal needs to be nurtured
          Are you my love desirous?
          Are you wanting, waiting?

Why wait till the stars are out so darn late
When all my nerves are frayed
          All our foreplay thus delayed
          Not to mention action somewhat staid

So as you please me, tease me
Longing ever more increase in me
          My mind conjures your gorgeous vision
          Our unity as if in most exotic mission

So let the early time set us in the mood
And our libido goes to fit our suit
          And in our love dance rollick and entertain
          With touch, embrace, feeling quite insane

So dear, let's share this pleasant measure
Together live and love is our treasure
          Fully conscious in this game we play
          And do it here and now, not wait for yet another day

~ ~ ~

Those who speak several languages
Also have more points of view
Regarding customs, and food,
But lovemaking—that is universal
And unrehearsed

She said "I forgot my pajamas!"
I said "That's OK, you can still sleep with me"
≈ ≈ ≈

Erotic Melody

Close relish of a snake dance
Embrace - hug, kiss
From every angle
Moment's ecstasy

The now, the It
Sweet luscious lips
Pressed so exotically
Touch mouth
Gently

Next pressed, deeply emotional
Middle finger - ever probing
A hundred kisses
Cheeks and neck
And forehead in many quarters

Delicious, delight
As heart jumps for joy
Eyes mesmerized and bulging
All concentrated on erotic body parts

The dance of love, experimental
Close, not callous, wriggling
Ever so close
Most inviting, participatory
As two bodies entwined

Teasing, touching, probing
Experimenting - each to heighten
The strong sense of nervous
Hormones jumping like a raucous
Brain and drum movement accompanied
By hand trumpets

The ecstatic dance of love, of union
Eager, erotic, willing, giving
The rapture of the moment
Until it too dissipates
And then rest close
Hug in unison
Two hearts
Forever

Men and women's chemistries differ but watch out when they mesh!

Mental Teen Dance

Frigid, frightened, he skirted
Away from she who flirted
And like an octopus embraced
Him, spinning his equilibrium laced

What once was a strong position
Now awkward, much indecision
Like frightened mouse or grouse
He'd rather hide in corner of his house

But closeness, chemistry of amour
A twosome dance a bit unsure
They hugged, they kissed
A certain distance she'd insist

For minutes together as one
Close, most electric feeling has begun
Into the hurricane called romance
Yet reticence not ready to engage in closest dance

So our young-lover minds bedazzled
Next day their vision with love frazzled
It's courting, sorting time, cavorting time
Does youth know how lucky they are in their prime?

Courtship

Should I write about what's best?
The bedroom conquest as bequest
Or flim-flam, bubble court
Test; "Is she the experimental sort?"

Please, not so verbose
You might cut off your nose
Or tongue sweet nothings most direct
Nor skip pontificate on every fact

Is it not jolly, free-spirited
To smile, joke, revert to clever kit
And wish that she responds in kind
At least some common ground we find

Sip body organs most impractical
Yet tease and talk position tactical
As secret bond as chemistry now sparks
I, balladeer, urge all to meet in parks

So she and I, drawn to this rendezvous
Without a chaperone or one of crew
Friendly sparks would lead to luscious kiss
Once projected who can miss?

And on the blanket cozy, under tent
She so agreeable and not resent
While with passion arms and legs
Precursor of a gold star for a little sex

≈ ≈ ≈

Await my love, my gorgeous delight
Enraptured, captured
She will enter my bedroom very soon.

Suspenders keep my pants up
Her bra is filled with many a cup
The gorgeous, high-heeled denied me
not
When we embraced said more, don't
stop!

Claw and Kiss

Kiss luscious lips, her face
Close arms cuddled, great embrace
A fervent missile filled with grace

Love each limb
Instant amour at a whim
Romantic, lights now dim

Tender touch
Squeeze each notch
Love so much

Meals - share
Salad - pear
Delicious fare

Lulled in lair
Really care
Suddenly suspicious scare

Memorized, adore
Kiss, tongue, fondle more
Infatuation tries to score

Intertwined, love connection
Glory grab with deep affection
Roaring right direction
Postpone parting; pain
Tears, attracted, sure to meet again
Just for now, memories sustain

Sex is here to stay; healthy, normal
An unlimited gift to pursue
And you may just die with a smile on your face

Wondering

Iridescent shimmer
 Wonder
  Soft fragrance of the night
   Teases me
    To know more
     Explore
      Out of my shell
       Into the light of moon
        I dwell
         Curious, excited
          Spirited — delighted
What could it be?
Who could it be?

Grandiose charm
 I am hesitant — feel inner alarm
  Somewhat tough
   I truly want to love
    Who is behind that shadow?
     Fascinating, attractive — do I know?
      Passionately I yearn
       Impatient let me learn
        Curiosity is incessant
Let me see you
Let me touch you
Let me love you
Let me ....

~ ~ ~

Flirtations, sex and fun are fine as long as there are no triangles

Casanova

In older age
Can you engage?
> Caught in love's unwitting tentacles
> Stirring emotion
> Long lost devotion

All nerves now reeling
Release your passion, intense feeling
> Dreamlike, new missions
> Desire, new decisions

Emotions perked and lifted
We are so lucky, so gifted
> Yet too busy to temper the notion
> Enticed undoubtedly by loving potion

And yet I cannot part
Old flames beat deep in my heart
> Yet this new flower
> Overpowers, exudes perfume

With little room to question – she is it!
Newfound heart flutters
Approbation, love terms uttered
> She so dear, so sweet, so kind
> Even when gone, she's still on my mind

Keep distance from the old flame (just the same)
If newfound heart is wonderful by any name
> Shower flowers and love calls morn and night
> I want to keep both lovers, but that simply is not right

For heart and soul
Directed, only one can make it whole
> She is my darling, I can relax
> Soon Lady X – no lack of sex
> And Lady Y, please, please don't cry

This is but a sample of life so complex
My world is dominated by sex
> You kid and joke – "It doesn't matter!"
> As well laid plans collapse and shatter

Who will it be?
Which one to see?
Oh, heaven help this Casanova hasbeen!

chapter twenty-three: american patriot

Patriot Act

Too often I contemplate and stare
Cognizant that life so unbalanced and unfair
Wonder, as I shake my head
Think deep and speculate before I go to bed
Digest the headlines, course of action
Lately, few leaders to my satisfaction

Our government now introducing strange new laws
Accomplishments are followed by guffaws
Elected to act noble – to protect and care
Self-adulation – empty message stripped so bare
Frustrated I shake my head
I want to run away instead

Fatigued, now close my eyes
Tomorrow's outline so unpredictable – no surprise
My mind now wanders to this day's great venture
Ups and downs with little censure
Leaders warn we're in some kind of war
Admonish us, "Be loyal – true to the core!"

Just into war, risk all I do not trust
These are games of war so bloody, full of lust
Investigates our lives? Our pocketbook?
Once committed where to look?
Search me, strip me, my privacy soon disappears
Obey and loyalty, First Amendment in arrears

Security – the watchword – reinforces power
Scare tactics and new edicts every hour
Guard bridges, highways, even schools
Billions spent; "security" now the golden rules

Imaginary enemy must now destroy
Do it cleverly, do it coy
Our leader in his role is out to win
The cause unsure, to kill is but a sin
Soon new election now at hand
Poor – rich – no one so fully understands
Brainwashed, no guts to demonstrate reject
Repetitious lies yes loyalty demands respect

Beguiled the zenith on Election Day
Elected! Self-righteous one – now here to stay
Biased leaders – fear of foreign threat
More false information the wily public fed
Caution and beware as ruling power leads
In self-adulation justifies their deeds – and needs

Creates new crisis to assert, retain more power
Solidifies commands to follow leader by the hour
He who is suspect – wrath of arrest
New holding prisons now attest
Jails, prisons and excommunication
Dismal pall hangs over nation

The wise men warned us long ago
That freedom price the truth to know
Unless the people vigilant – democracy decay
So vote, express, protest –inform in every way
Your democratic voice must blend
The power grabbers soon will understand

But once, a Mussolini, Hitler, Stalin it's too late
The propaganda certifies your guilt and fate
Future and dreams and hopes turned sour
Unruly dictator exerts his power
I cringe and cry, shed many a tear
Yes, in truth it can happen right here

Too late, I shake my head

Colin Powell

Last year I sat next to Colin at a dinner. He gave me his autobiography and I, in turn, gave him one of my poetry books. Several weeks later, after reading part of my book he sent a personal handwritten note and thanked me.

Between loyalty and conviction
This great man blessed in speech and diction
Bridged boundaries of color and race
Now worldwide we admiringly honor his face

General of incredible renown
Admired, respected in each American town
He's considerate, deliberate, and wise
Eventual nominee for Nobel Prize

A gracious nation gives him thanks
He advanced, attained our nation's highest ranks
At each turn bridged opportunity and fate
During critical time became U.S Secretary of State

His country now in dual war
No victory in sight, body bags now counted by the score
His values honorable, but made a big mistake
Issues of war and peace at stake

Upright and loyal to Bush, the President
Bush's principles he proudly did defend
Yet greatness constantly weighs and tests
Conflicts among the very best

War and weapons of mass destruction?
In front of US Assembly proudly claimed such production
(Most of us felt a story of concoction)
Now he confesses he was duped?
Damage of declaring war can never be recouped

Resulted in invasion of Iraq
At first successful, lots of luck
Many did challenge, most despaired
Positive reports by the President were aired

Only future history will weigh
His place is in the limelight of today
From high position and high station
Powell's job, to safeguard our nation

Weapons of Mass destruction?
He waffled at U.N. with weak delivery and conviction
Never took a stand at interdiction
Years later he admitted his mistake
Apologized, Sadat, he said, still a rake

Sad, but true, this great man, Colin Powell
We do not pretend
The country, desperate, needed a man on whom it could depend
He blew it, truly could have been a great President

Colin Powel, Judy Weil (daughter) and Arthur

They say your home is your castle,
but what about the mortgage, taxes,
maintenance, and utilities?
Turtles have it lucky.

We March

Mostly we slither, walk or crawl
Cajole, rejoice, and blatantly brawl
This time
         We march
In unison
Though not in step

         We march
For justice, fairness
For moderation, not excess (unless)
For nature's preservation
Self-destructive, the planet's population
We march for babies loved and cared
For old, crippled pain diminished and spared
For science and research
Disease, sicknesses we must purge

         We march
For hope, for belief of fellow man
Fortuitous share our lifetime span
For less desire in material things
For feelings equal to the leaders and kings
For less vanity
For less insanity

         We march
For the arts
The painter, poet, wrlter
Musician, singer, soul-enlightener
For the of show of athletes great
We hail the icons, shout their fate
Icons with money, riches
Dazzle us, performance stars
For them, with them
         We march

We march
Most of all for will and cause
Our belief balances, better loves
Lucky in a sea of freedom's air
We can express, partake and dare
We are tiny ants on mankind's giant globe
The actors, protagonists of hope

We march
As symbols, flags of voice
We march to change society
Provide some choice
We march to right some wrong
We know the world so small
Can be so much better

We march
Together
Into the unending horizon
One step at a time

Occupy?

I don't live in a tent
Part of the everyday 99%
But in my heart I too occupy
Perturbed, precarious nation
Leaders ambivalent and anti-compromise

Poor schoolchildren denied
Welfare women restricted
Diminished services for sick and elderly
"We can't afford it
While those who deny live lofty
Not yet gnawed by hunger, cold and no roof"

To protest, demonstrate
First Amendment - peaceably
Healthy youth, aged, homeless
Misfits - all
Veterans, anarchists, more than a right
Ignorance, inaction left a vacuum

In tents or on the square
Peacefully or under arrest, regain respect
Have the rich pay their share
For teachers, police, research, infrastructure
Legislate before it's too late
You bankers atone for your greed!

As profits mount for the 1%
We can't all be hypocrites
Where is the fairness?
Where is the justice?
Where is the future, our tomorrow?

Obstinate republicans, contrary democrats
Rather than compromise, let legislation die
Nothing, nothing- a vacuum while the country bleeds
Stubborn: Better let the patient die
Fragment the inevitable

Living Memorial Sculpture Garden, Weed, Northern California

Do you hear us?
You can see us -
And we can see you too!
I really don't have to occupy you
I am a resident
I am here to stay
Can you see and hear me now?

≈ ≈ ≈

Rigid, rough, ready
Political minority party
In their attack
Not sanctimonious
By strong leadership to make their point
To hell with the country
Did you say Democracy?

237

America

I, the immigrant, recount our history
Amazed at this band of
Early revolutionaries
Imbued with a new spirit of freedom;
Thomas Paine, Alexander Hamilton
Adams, Washington, Jefferson
Such preordained, educated gentlemen
In the pursuit of happiness
Bedded in ideas of independence
Rough land of colonizers

Tiny cities
Philadelphia, Boston New York, Savannah,
Virginia Farmers, plantation owners
Such rich fabric of pioneers
Tilling the rough fields in Massachusetts, Rhode Island
Fishing in New England
And harvesting tobacco on the plantations
Of the Carolinas, Georgia
From Alexander Hamilton
To Washington's soldiers, ambassadors
The maneuvers to get France on our side

Supplies, valor, pride, sacrifice, 1776
Leadership, cowardice
Men of new lands
To risk all
Wealth, name, citizenship
Christian and others, Quakers, dialects
Their letters, their muscles
Their words, their sacrifice in an uncertain time
Steeped in English tradition, English laws
King George III and Parliament dominate
Dared test the unjust laws
Brilliantly contributed by punishing patriots

Ideas hew the words of The Declaration of Independence
Our Constitution and our Bill of Rights
This spirit transcends
Into my blood I, the immigrant kid
Whose dire ancestors traded
With Indians 30 years later
A fellow named Emmerich
My great-great-great grandfather
Partner of John Jacob Astor
Indian Trader from Germany
More than a century later
I escaped from Nazi Germany
Tasted Chicago's wild freedom
Delivered The Sun Times
Sold shoes, struck behind
Green grocer Hillman
Two way ticket to WWII U.S. soldier, translator
G.I. Bill – B.A. M.A. teacher
Rewarded by Uncle Young ex-G.I.

No car, simple studio apartment
Paid rent on time
Girlfriend – 17, I was 21
Inexperienced courted by streetcar
Movies, dancing, concerts
Elaine, slim, dark, high-heeled
Well-proportioned breasts
Total freedom I live alone, no siblings
Father dead
No one gave a damn but me
Education – history Teacher – that's me!
A sometime human being!
Now a writer with grandchildren
An armchair philosopher
Pragmatic, a believer
Skeptic about the world
I dig those early American revolutionaries
Their uncanny wisdom
My stepping stone today

chapter twenty-four: food and other addictions

Licorice, The Devil

Box almost emptied
10 pieces of black licorice
Sweet, sugary
Into my blackened mouth

        I industrially chew madly, in bed
        Five more black pieces left
        Hungry tongue tasting, I devour
        This late hour 1:22 a.m.

Now in my gnawing stomach
Churns black snakes of licorice
Will my blood turn black?
My brain takes orders from an avaricious devil

        I chew; I can't desist
        Like a chain smoker, Stop! Resist!
        Time! Sleep time –
        God, let me sleep in peace!
        There's just one more box waiting

~ ~ ~

Too many cookies
Can fill the stomach
And nauseate the mind.

Mouthwatering Gift

My toast is seared
  Begs to be devoured
   Fruit of the earth
    Aromatic, brown grains
     Crusty, uneven
      Spread light butter
       Best with sweet, chunky strawberry jam
        Savor each bite upon bite
         Toasty, texture over tongue
          The total taste
           Teased flavor inhaled through nostrils
           Swallow, bite to my heart's delight
            And think —
             Ah, the wonderful tangible things
              More promises ahead
               Such joy from such simple
                Splendid bread
                 Crunch, crunch
                Satisfied for now with this abundance
               Hardly can contain myself
              Only 14 more hours to go
             And I can feast again
            Carry on where I left off —
           Push aside those artificial, material treasures
          Nothing compares to this remarkable
         Mouth-watering gift!

Like It Or Not

So if you like it now
Will you like it later?
How much?
And as a signal in the brain says
"I like it,
          I like it,
                    I like it"

I trip and fall

          d
           o
            w
             n
              s
               t
                a
                 i
                  r
                   s

                         ≈ ≈ ≈

Delectable, delicious,
          divine
The feast invites like
colors of the rainbow
     To be devoured
     Greatest the joy
     before the meal
     Especially on an
     empty stomach

Food and other addictions

There is no doubt, IT CAN BE DONE. At eighty-seven years old, five foot six, I bend over and barely see my shoes. For forty-five years I weighed a slim 145 pounds. From a school teaching job to a latent, lazy, chair-ridden realtor, I soon boomed to 185 pounds for the next forty years. Oh, did I enjoy feasts, noshing late at night, while being somewhat inactive all those years. Being an avid theater-goer, some of the best local restaurants became my downfall. A touch of diabetes put the scare in me, so I took an eight week "MOVE ON" course at the Veteran's Administration, cashing in some rewards from my World War II foreign service. As a novice, here were some positive lessons I took from the course. It's all an attitude. Understanding calories, ingredients, salt and sugar intake. One has to learn to say, "No! This is not healthy for my intake".

1. Resist, avoid, and seek a more positive alternative. So, staring at the bakery counter, I quickly reject the teasing donuts, fritters, turnovers...
2. It's an absolute "no" to Coke, soda, sweet bottled drinks and juices, all so appetizing, but no longer on the list. Fresh fruit; "yes!" An apple or pear a day, for instance. There is always mixed fresh salad, wonderful; the myriad of fresh vegetables and fruits beckoning to be devoured.
3. Again, "No" to simple white bread, potatoes, rice, all of which turn into sugar.
4. Simultaneous exercise. Be it walking a half hour a day, biking, swimming, treadmill, or simple physical activity for ten to thirty minutes daily; a must!
5. In spite of the fact that I love soups, I discovered that these "healthy" soups carry a very high dose of salt and often are rich in cream.
6. MOVE ON taught me to serve myself small portions, or to leave some food on the plate. Eat slowly and chew well. Put your fork down often and of course drink lots of water.
7. A glass of water an hour before eating helps reduce hunger. Also, it takes 20 minutes after eating before your stomach signals a full dose. Enough is enough! So stop eating BEFORE you feel full (use Google; there many more healthy tricks to forestall hunger).
8. Get support from friends, family or spouse. As great as eating out is, it puts on far too many calories from the excess butter, salt and other fats, though the taste may be exemplary.
9. Over and over, it's the rejection, refusal, the saying to yourself, "No". This self-control is paramount to your success.
10. I weigh myself naked at the same time every day (morning is best, first thing) and in the last 8 weeks am down from185 to 175 pounds. It isn't all water loss, and I feel lighter, stronger and more mobile. I should loose at least five more pounds.
11. Find a reward system for your small, important goals. Buy yourself something special; a healthy snack or some personal treat that you cherish.
12. As you would for an addict (no drugs, alcohol in the house), similarly, why tempt yourself with soft drinks, sweets, candy, cookies, ice-cream? Out! Give or throw them away. Losing weight is mind over matter. Doesn't your health matter?

If an "old honkey" like me can do it over time, so can you! It's not luck, it's the determination to live longer and healthier.

Love Me

"Love Me,"
Starved, she cried out
"Love me, love me!"
Dissipated, drunken lover's bout
Only the TV blared, flickering light
In the dark, dingy, disjointed room
A sigh, a haunting voice:
"Love me, love me."
Followed by another futile diminishing whimper.

No answer.

Bed unmade, kitchen squalor
Negligence, a scruffy cat
In a corner the dirty litter box
Stale smell of beer permeates the air
Empty whisky bottle
Dark dreary stains on the rug
Newspaper scattered

It's only 8:32 PM
Tears, whimper,
"Love me."
In a stupor she lies on her smudged bed cover
A hopeless vision
Lost in space and time
"Love me!" a tearful expression

Now with a whimper she drowns in her own tears.
Finally a total silence
Only someone in outer space is listening.

∼ ∼ ∼

We all have bad habits
And it's all our parents' fault

Rummage Sale

After painful, solid sorting I now start
Great piles of goods I will now impart
Old pots and pans
A bunch of toys worth just a glance
Knick-knacks and rags
Desks, ornate cabinets marked with tags
Thousands of ties, men's shirts
Woman's shoes, dresses and skirts

>Outgrown trousers, suits
>Tight, slightly worn boots
>Videos, outdated electrical junk
>*Ashamed to what level I had sunk*
>All these things discarded, will not adorn
>Long time ago paraded, suited, not often worn
>Donate books on health, on sex and fiction
>So factual read without the dereliction

All stuffed into bags and every kind of box
Not to forget cases of old socks
Good deal, should sell soon without fail
At this monumental annual cancer rummage sale
All the goodies did reflect my life, my past
Recognize their uselessness, nothing will last
I feel my addiction parting with this treasure
Have to get rid of much at every leisure

>Grand housecleaning to a happy tune
>The money goes for worthy cause - cancer cure real soon
>Once out of house, look at all the extra space
>All part of freer living in this human race
>So lucky, *rid of the anchor of so much stuff*
>You know darn well at home you too have enough
>Away with extras as you do reflect and pause
>Feel good, feel happy, all went to a heavenly cause

For while I am alive, I do not deprive
No goodies, junk in afterlife
Just lucky to have love, and friends
And peace to satisfy and make amends
So careful if you're burdened with too many things
Just have your necessities, stay free
There's more to do and more to see

Ingredients

Ingredients should have a touch of love
Make a brilliant mixture
With blessings from above
In every heart this feeling should be a fixture
The dish is rich and so inviting,
Tantalizing nerves and senses
Taste buds and tongue, it's so exciting
Overeat with consequences.
So relish and partake while food is waiting
And forget the critic and the measure
Eat to your heart's content without abating
Lucky to devour this tasty treasure

∻ ∻ ∻

Here's a hint:
Don't be fascinated by the chocolate mint in your mouth –
it will quickly disappear but now you're hooked for life

Chocolate Addict

Hershey's milk chocolate
So tasty at 4AM – gives me a rush
Small chocolate bites as I chew
Each swallow, another aphrodisiac

    Cocoa beans and sugar cubes
    Sweet, tasty into hatch of mouth
    More silence, chew, saliva chemistry in action
    As mouth gyrates, moves up and down, I swallow

And chocolate blindly melts in mouth
Tear and unwrap, break off another piece
Then another, overdosed I spell my doom
Sugar, cocoa, butter in right proportions

    Can't see the brown dissolve in warm inviting mouth
    Juggled by my tongue
    But taste buds dance so delighted
    Each swallow a corrupt hypnotic enjoyment

Taste into whirl, chin and muscles most erratic
As is every aspect of my moving mouth
While tongue and saliva, chocolate
Do their trick

    A simple piece of candy for the ages
    A chocolate addict in remission

~ ~ ~

A dirty car
Shows a problematic owner
(me)

*There are so many
addictive vices
Lucky me! I have
only two or three of
them*

Visions of dice cast six and four
An arbitrary decent score
To gamble, dare, some say a sin
Our wage we risk and only sometimes win
Remember gambling does not bring fame
It's purely an exciting, expensive game

*Drugs, drink, overeat
Some bad stuff often will repeat
Like a driven animal you self-destruct
Into torturous hell be sucked*

Every day something good happens (we live)
and something we'd rather not talk about...

It's OK to goof off, be wasteful at times
Makes you feel powerful, strong, enriching
Soon to be dragged back to old routines
Careful, it may become habit forming

Sometimes I just want to hibernate
And hide behind myself

If it's no good, double it
And it will still be no good; so take a hike

A little appetite
and a
little appetite
add up to

....gluttony

I like candy
Candy likes me
We keep our dentist busy

chapter twenty-five: enjoy the arts

Drowning in great creativity,
from music to stage to fine art

How lucky, at my tender age of 87, to partake twice weekly in the great art forms here in the Bay Area near San Francisco and Berkeley. I am dazzled by live theater (over forty choices weekly!), great orchestras, opera and super musicals, all enjoyed by me from the center seats. Museums, art exhibits and galleries are available readily. Oh, what mental feasts abound to enrich and stimulate !

Take time out to admire the display of talent and art forms around you of every kind. Be it baroque music, great oratorios, native music, the world's greatest symphonies and ballets all at your fingertips. The classics, Shakespeare, Broadway productions and famous live speakers all fill my insatiable appetite. There are always second balcony cheap seats, online or last minute offers, or standing room for some shows too. You could even usher and enjoy hundreds of performances free.

Creativity in the form of the arts is all around us. Slowly our American civilization is coming into its own. European nations have long been the backbone of the arts. Classical music, opera, English theater, French and Dutch paintings, European culture, architecture, you name it. Each wave of American immigrants contributed (and still contribute today) to our Nation's melting pot of culture, particularly in literature and movie making. Though still at the edge of modernity compared to Europe or the Chinese and Japanese civilizations, for example, we relish and value our art forms just as much, often with fewer government grants which are so common in Europe and Asia.

IMPRESSIONISTS: A MENTAL HIGH!

I thrill at the dim painting's reflection
Cezanne, Monet, Degas, Van Gogh and turn to observe
The fantastic oils, their colorful brush strokes
That adorn the walls of the world's galleries
Each to the beholder; the skilled, educated, artist
I am in wonder, full of admiration
Of their talents

Inches away I focus, strenuously, on the color
The action, the movement, the angles
Of those great impressionist painters
Each making an imprint unique for me

My brain, like a digital camera,
Records and stores somewhere upstairs
In my gray cells
So I can spot the picture's artist from afar
Over and over as I enter new and old galleries

Those paintings lift my spirits,
In awe, I thank God and nature
For the opportunity to admire
Pissarro, Seurat, Gauguin

They are certainly my friends,
My visages, my dreams, inspirations
With their moods and bursts of
color
Embedded in my mind forever
Mine to behold and reassure

Music

A thousand nerve fibers
Transmit to my inner ear
Absorb the soft sound
Musical, melodious, dear
Shuffle my feelings
Make my heart pound
Like musical food
I, human, lucky to receive
To transcend – the beat, the rhythm
Translate – the joy, the melody
Complicated magic
Pluck the senses
My soul restored
I almost swoon; sing along
Pick out my favorite record
Hum in tune
Sophisticated, stimulating
My body sways to the winds
The melody lingers
The beat embeds in my mind
Even my heartbeat drumming
Rich oxygen fluid shimmies
Through my veins
Tonal shades of love, moods
New dimensions
Calm; earth and moon
Feelings leaping
Sound waves waltzing
Spread to all extremities
Dance lightly in flight
You and I will become one

≀ ≀ ≀

Why can't I be an actor
When all of us really are,
Since all the world is our stage?

Canvas of life

Like a painter with his easel, colors,
At first stroke on the blank canvas
So, we create our life in all its hues and colors
From birth the many textures,
The bride of happiness,
Dreams and plans ahead
The struggle to maintain values
Right and wrong, the language,
Deed and doing

>The *dark gray* of gloomy disappointment
>The relaxed *green* of growth and change
>The *purples and violets* have their place
>The *azure blue* of ocean, sea and sky
>These are the elements we live in and with
>They surround us, give us our playing field

Yet, when we're older,
Still the canvas is incomplete.

The bright array of *rainbow colors* a bit faded
Still rich, dazzling, dancing, impressionistic
Some call it existence, some the splendor of life
Some in their flashy ways and clothes
Others disheveled, but all by now find opportunities missed

Life is a self-portrait - a merger of the times
A fusion
Some of us make our own fate
Our health, intelligence and stature
But for much of life, you are in the driver's seat
Limited to your territory, yet adventurous

And you get to pick
Your *colors*

Life's a STAGE

A good show can never last too long,
Be it bloody drama or siren song,
Or ninth inning of a tied game,
Or fourth quarter score all the same,
Or good loving, passionate, intense,
Or an unexpected romp that does not make sense.

All this is to satisfy my want,
Fool, dart hither and thither in the pond.
Release from duty, entertain,
Keep my senses, could easily go insane!
Ahhh, if my life could be an active stage,
Just before curtain down in riveting rage.

But first, I must dress my torso,
Rush to the theater in finery
ever more so
Sometimes bored, some-
times fascinated.
Be participant, observer,
know how the end is fated,
Trigger joy in mind and
much pleasure.
Many happy memories
I treasure!

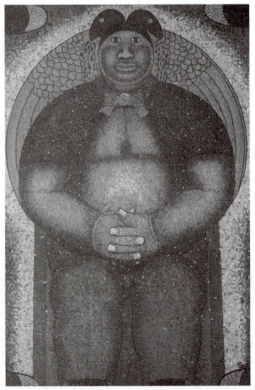

So now plan,
Attentive participant,
Curtain's up,
But don't be late...

Benny Bufano mosaic mural,
Oakland, CA

254

A Wonderful Day

If you can still see
The vast panorama
Like an artist's pallet of colors
All the hues of green, browns and blue
An overwhelming endless canvas
Of brooks, trees, meadows
All meeting the aqua blue unending sky
An open vista of dazzling colors
So true, so real, beholden

Eyes open, there is a flock of blackbirds
The murmur of a stream tumbling
Some nearby trees rustle
It is a pastoral, peaceful canvas
Ever to be explored until embedded in your soul

As we walk within the painting
We feel freedom, openness
A minor miracle overcome, obsessed
The gravity and power of nature to stimulate
Or to relax, rest and meditate
As with each waking step we inhale
The fresh breeze caressing our cheeks
"It's a wonderful day,
Isn't it?"

≈ ≈ ≈

Each man has his own language
Never to forget the words
But often the meaning

Chorus

All fingers in the chorus point at me
I can't read a single note, you see
I love the music, and can kind of sing
A rich basso voice to chorus bring

Alto, not tenor voice or bass
The echo signifies, pitch in right place?
Brass vocal bark, no good, I fear
That I do or don't belong right here

Two thousand eyes now fixed on me
I feel a bit scared, must go and pee
Do love music, did nothing wrong
Dressed formal, now in the chorus, where I belong!

Could mute my words, mouth the whole project
Too devious, yet a challenge for my intellect
I also learned to keep a timely beat
Talents inspirational with hands and feet

Yet, if you can distinguish someone out of tune
It's not me; it's the clown on the other side of the room!

To be exposed
Is to be undressed
In front of an audience.
Like it or not,
Cover it up
Or ham it up

On Stage

From the time I wake
I perform;
What clothes to wear?
Which words to use?
And which to avoid?

Who directs?
What guides the following buzz?
Questions unanswered...

Just a moment!
I reflect, I am amazed
More thoughts bombard my days
Never "finish"
Writer, actor
Me, the protagonist
We all
All of us
From early morn
Protagonist extra-ordinary!

Constantly, we are
On Stage

≈ ≈ ≈

*Believers and dreamers
can see invisible colors and vibes
that skeptics cannot see.*

Theater of Life

In 5 minutes
        So many seconds
                The curtain comes up
And my gray cells   alert   anticipate
The rip roaring begins
        I'm fastened to my seat
                With each scene and ambiance I inhale
                        Torrents of words and sentiment
                                Slang, music, voice, antics all
                                Tickle my mind

Actors
        m   e   l   t
        Shaped in the illusion
                Of tangible reality.
                        They torment my innocence and activate guilt
                        Author and actor collaborate
                        A biopsy of life

I hear, witness identify
        Emphasize, concur and disagree
                The climax waits - hushed for my anticipation
                        Eyes riveted, ears cocked
Applause
        La Fin
                Curtain Down
                Period.
                        Enriched, I leave the theater,
My emotion unfulfilled
        Ready to explore my life.
                I, the protagonist,
                    Bow to you.

If you can stand good humor
Then you can stand good art,
As your body shakes inside out
Laughing at the contradictions

Speaker

Sadly, today's luncheon speaker
Not an information "leaker"
Rattles, reads in monotone
Boring, dry, I can but moan
Reviewers, orators, those who teach
Please, do not just read your speech
Give a forceful intro, gesture, and postulate
Be descriptive, entertain and demonstrate
Audience glued, to most important factor
In your speech do intonate and be an actor
And to think I paid for this affair
Let me disappear and imagine I wasn't there

I don't know why we must wear underwear all the time...

Adam and Eve didn't and they almost got along.

chapter twenty-six:
an old man's meanderings

Space Between Earth and Sun

The spirit drenched
He who faces nothingness
Frustration, an empty heart, numb
Ready to jump
Who wants to blow his own brain to smithereens?

Forget the code of life
Unlock the gates of heaven –
If there be a heaven
Empty battery, nil life value
How did he survive all these years?
Onslaught of laugher and of tears
Has lived, experienced, and yet feels
Yes feels, there is nothing now to live for
Out of the window, the years of hope and faith
Now victim of the agony and pain of self-defeat
Last straw – no more
No more failures
No more tranquilizers
No more baiting, demoralizing pain
The ugly chuckle, laugh of ridicule
The mockery of ill, and that of fool
Write notes of love, love to all
There is discomfort – wait for devil's call

Anyway to choke
Or bullet pierces – poor bloke
As poison cramps, the body stilts
Blank nothingness

No light – the sun shines somewhere
But here in this darkness, no shadow
Waves crash, the earth trembles
Avalanches, floods and forest fires
Shrill noise drowns out the tranquil music
Depressed, spineless sufferer of daily blues
I ask you with concern and fear
Life? Not heaven's gift to hold so dear?
Can I escape? Escape to what?

So what is left?
You can guess…
Simply nothing
The space between earth and sun
A void aching to be filled!

Old People

Old people are like children
Determined, obstinate, daring
Dogged, suspicious
What is there to lose?
The eternal spring of self
And self-delusion

In value of time
Life is still a playground
Why not romp and play
And let the devil
Hang himself

Time is the greatest treasure
Wisely to be spent
But it slips, disappears in flashes
But there is so much, much more
Before the heavy eyes close

A Lifetime

We wave good-bye to childhood toys
Like robin's wings - escapes the nest, enjoys
In growth, we too experiment and search
As stimulated youth satisfies the investigative urge
So does the bird build his own nest
While others roam the continents to celebrate their fest
Feed on curiosity and drive to satisfy desire
To conquer, taste and set the world on fire.

Mementos are stored, succumb in a small abode
Yet many collectibles we unnecessarily unload
Some custom jewelry, braided cloth, and letters...
Tons of pictures and film display the story of our betters
The remnants; a frayed old man and woman's glasses
The ordinary, insignificant, so common to the masses
Still coherent, waiting for the latest news
Outside their door the ever-busy street-cleaning crews

In simple, silent dresser, bed and a chair
The latest necessities for which we care
Too soon, in time our souls and memories forgotten
Good things remembered, erase the negative and rotten
And the last good-bye, hospital or cemetery
Still bright bundles of remembrances that we carry
Drowned out by the loud and busy day
The old destroyed for new, must now make way

Graveyards become housing projects, to please the eye
Too soon. Too soon!   Good-bye, good-bye.

∼ ∼ ∼

There is never enough time –
So be brilliant, and use well the precious time you have.
Once gone, never to return.

Stay A While

Cranky, contrite, almost crying
Old hermit harried not yet dying
Reflects in his sculpture, shape and age
When handsome, young,   was quite the rage

Now withered, wilted, wounded, weary
Creature of contrasts and quite dreary
Athletic prowess in his skeleton demised
Over eons to weary worn-out years   smaller sized

No more the rabble rousing, rough player
Coy curmudgeon or soothsayer
Shattered own successful, discriminate codes
Rescued many in most   unsavory modes

In higher circles still in solid, stern demand
His enemies succumb with helping hand
And so portrayed perchance someone recognizes
With honors for the well-earned   people's prize

Amazed, not phased, a painter's smile
Thank god this earth now lets him

                                                  stay
                                                  a
                                                  while

Sick

Sick with the flu, miserable, I rationalize
The world has stopped
Nose dripping, sinus headache
Sore throat
Deserve it or not, I am in misery!
I am out of commission
It's someone else's turn
To save the world

No Time Out

We all wonder
Scrutinize and ponder
How much of me I saved
The elements I braved

What, where to eat
What magazines to read
The idiotic little things
For commoners and even kings

In honesty, so busy that I run
Events unfurl—some duties and much fun
Collage, confused the total scene
Obtuse, often forget where I have been

Destructive news warns on the phone
My enemy so near did clone
Friend diagnosed, now radiation
Cancerous, mortal - next station

Rush to fill my daily list
Much humanness busy, something's missed
Fanatic focus on my goal
Often missed magic parts of the big whole

So now will set aside the quality and special time
To kiss a mother or child's cheek is not a crime
Inhale the fragrant air of bloom
And in my heart for much more joy make room

We blast barnstorming through life
Only at a few momentous, maniacal moments
Do we stop to carefully collate
Only to rush on and on
Until only marvelous, moist memories are left.

Forget

Some are meticulous, never forget
You often beget, always regret
Then there are things you'd rather never get
Can't erase them out of your head
Until the brain is so fully loaded
Guilt, anxiety, almost exploded
Best ease the pain, take your time
You'll be fine
You'll see...
Unless you're as forgetful as me

The more I learn and know,
the more I learn what I don't and will never know
And that, I leave to Google

Breeze Into the Night

Breeze, breeze into the night
Or early morn beckons so bright
Yet sometime time and life do disappear
Lost, squandered what we hold most dear

Hold that moment memory in mind
Hold it lovingly and life will then
Be kind

It's yours alone to hold
Can't be bought nor sold
Safe haven in your soul
To heal and make the wound now whole

You, whole ecstatic in your prime
Relive this feeling "to the end of time."

DOORS

Imagine yourself, your life
Which doors have you entered?
Ah, so many each and every day
Do you see the doors?

> From space to space
> In the privacy of our homes
> The bathroom, basement and attic
> Doors that hold secrets

You know you can enter or exit
Unsure of what you might find
Parents' young, bidding
Full of love, endearing

> Doors of many colors
> Great hopes
> Openings of fear, frustration
> Doors I never want to enter again

Doors once opened
Part of my youth
(If you play with pet birds
Never leave the door open)

> Doors are merely extensions of
> Our boxed-in lives
> Doors of separation, of sound
> Of smell, of life

Truly, doors are not natural
Where in the mountains and valleys
The expanse of open meadows
Do you see doors?

> *I like to reinvent myself*
> *But I am limited to few materials*

Old Man's Meandering

No jubilation or laudatory clap
I witness his dribble dastard drab
Of odd old man's meandering mind
Coherent contentious pieces find
The world's going to hell and a piss pot
With famine, dry spell, let all soothsayers rot

Lived exited four score years and more
Experienced so much, it'll make you sore
Sometimes intolerant to open thought of mind
Doomsday philosophers of any kind
Warns of excess waste and egocentric acts
Wakes our world, too busy, no time to relax

Like the parsimonious, secure my nest
In wisdom follow hunches for what's best
Respect and love my foremost goal
Exemplify life's true values is my role
When to say "yes," when to say "no"
When to wing it or respect the pro

So in these precious upper years
Live gently, with my friends and peers
Silvery strands, crags, weather-beaten face
Recline with well-earned dignity and grace
And when perchance all clicks so smooth
Be thankful for the joy and freedom yet to choose

Just let me be...

I am a silly everyman
Who wants to, if he could and can
Who languishes and laughs about
And, wobbly, wings above the crowd
I flutter with the butterflies
Honey dripping tear-drops in my eyes
Regardless of season, reason, sun or rain
Each day anew I'm born again

And when I see a damsel sweet
I brush my shoes so very neat
Alas, rejected, still feel scattered
Damsel ignores me, as if it really mattered
At times, if only the world would let me alone
I'd scamper, pamper and atone
I am a contemplative creature of routine
I come, I go, I'm never, ever a has-been

So tease me, squeeze me
Don't appease me
Just follow my decree
Which says, "Just let me be!"

Electric Shock

Treatment Tomorrow - unhappy victim
Eye of the storm
On gurney towards an operating room
I see the white antiseptic hospital hall
Blank white wall, white ceiling
As I am rolled in.
Greeted by smiling cheerful nurses
Each at their station, trained ritual
Eerie tentacle equipment
From a modern space age.
Intravenous nodes
Mind still focused on my heart procedure.
Imagine, for seconds
Out cold - temporarily dead
My heart experiences an electrical shock
So powerful as to restore
While my limp body floats in air
Tries to get my heart rhythm to normal.
Or so invasive
That my thinned blood will reach every nerve ending
Off to my brain, deliver less oxygen
Make me a half-fulfilled
Old creature of our demented society.
Why not call me tomorrow after 5pm?
Maybe then I'll know my future
For every person is linked to the next
And my future is yours, too.

I Should Have Been Dead Long Ago!

Caveat - should have been long dead
Yet in old age, jovial, I jump around instead
Amidst the joy all watch, all the convoluting new
So mystified, hilarious, tainted by the witches brew

I've done it all, seen it all
Risen high, then had my fall
I've courted, bonded, loved like crazy
Most diligently active, at times was lazy

Suffered in my own creation
A valiant, loyal soldier for this nation
Proud that my kids like an arrow hit their mark
Shows worthy life with pizzazz and much spark

Lived through lonely lousy rough times
Fought off array of devil's curse and rhymes
Survive global warming, smell the rancid air
Dreamer: time to phase out wars with their despair

Now I wallow, think of my dear old dog
Miss the warmth, eager look, now dead like rock
Earned rich, rewards - little surprise
Defeated, deflated, now regain and rise

And now aged, time left even less
Less meaning for the things I now possess
I want to share, to love, to be with you, dear friend
A free-spirited hermit – experience all until the very end.

～ ～ ～

They say I am young at heart – I wish they
would tell that to my bones

chapter twenty-seven:

words that fly

Words – the power of explosives

Nothing to be afraid of
Words – only words
So easily said
Like a cold that turns into pneumonia
Orders, messages, communication
However when the giver's tongue is acid
"J'accuse" as Emile Zola said
Or the Federalist Papers
Or the Gettysburg address
Or Remember the Maine
Or when Mr. Collin Powell
Mirrored George Bush's words
And promoted the idea of weapons of mass destruction
Words unleashed resulted into a costly Iraq war
Words now can easily have the power of explosives
Words take on the venom of hate
Even when mother scolds there are consequences
So that all hell can break loose
Or listen to the new savior
Who preaches his only true new religion
To save mankind unless you want to be doomed
Or the liar who bears false witness
Condemning the innocent
And imagine all this in hundreds of different tongues

Too long a monologue turns the listener off
Unless he is a prisoner

Word Blitz!

Fair-haired, fruitcake and fertilizer
Digested, arrested
Released, pleased, eased
In your own world
Solicitous, singular, insincere.

Crab apple, kangaroo, coyote
Desperate, desired, delicious, deranged
Gargantuan, gregarious, gorgeous
Languid, lazy, luxurious, lax
Curvaceous, candid, crying, caring.

Wild, witty, welcome, winsome, whenever
Scary, sculptured, serpentine, sensational
Funnel, fabulous, fruitful, fortuitous
Tired, tepid, tedious, tender, troubled.

Meet by the ocean's shore, ocean floor
Fried fish food, fandangle, fetish, fabulous
Marvelous meals, Mardi Gras melody
Devilish, delectable, adorable, darling.

A non-entity of nonsense, a potpourri of nothing
Spellbound, solicitous, solemn
Ubiquitous, loyal, loving, living
Enchanted, enriched and ever lasting.

~ ~ ~

The ego feeds the urge to write
Expands my being day and night
Share wisdom and my inner thought
My being never sold or bought.
I pour out treasure troves within
I feel you close, just let me in.

271

An Ode to My Pen

Between my index finger and thumb
A precious pen immobile, dumb
Until, directed by my brain
This gifted instrument in dance again
In spirited circles and gyrations
Pens mark inordinate sensations

> "I love you, miss you" now in tune
> The rhapsody of love begins to swoon
> Or bitter words:" I'm so ashamed"
> All the while I know I'm framed!
> On paper soon the soul pours out
> A litany of feelings from the fountain spout

And oh, once written, kind and unkind dribble so embossed
The receptor ready in all anger challenge tossed
The written accusations in red dripping ink
A warning for the bare-knuckled bout in bloody rink
Once on computer carefully announced
The critic's hammer and some proudly pounced

> Ah, so much do I like and love my pen
> Again, again and then again, I am its most avid fan
> With this sharp tool, I pour out my greatest wish
> Or drool; send out written recipe of favorite dish
> Too many bills, in debt up to my neck
> Pen will soon help me write and pay with a check

It was the pen that crafted our Constitution
Or freedom's manifesto that proclaimed the revolution
Or Homer, Plato, Aristotle with the stroke of a pen
Their wisdom mark made us their eternal fan
Or when Karl Marx or Engel, with pen proclaimed
Communist manifesto in which workers are framed

Or chronicles from kingdoms past
The history of most promiscuous cast
Or Vatican libraries exploding with the pen's art
For pen, word and mind are never far apart
I reiterate, I simply love my pen and its strength
My deepest feelings written at great length

 Ecstatic, I communicate
 I sign documents, I even sign my fate
 The words like thrashing waves express
 My past, my now, my wishes to possess

Each pen at master's bidding so profound
Sincere and honest scribbling do abound
Sometimes a smudge shows writer's tears
Most often greetings from close dears
And sometimes writings are so grotesque
Embarrassed not to meet the tests and requests

 And oh, when Kugelschreiber suddenly turns blank
 Another pen replaces at first rank
 The execution now on paper does proclaim
 Washington, Jefferson and Lincoln's name
 Or writer's autograph, one from a movie star
 The egotist will share his writings wide and far

Oh yes, I love my pen
Can hardly wait again
To sit at valley's riverside
Compose the lovely sonnets for my bride
Or in autobiography describe my life in great hilarity
With pen a touch left to posterity.

 No matter which mood I'm in, the pen is at my bidding
 It will record compliments or naughty verses at each sitting
 Or if downhearted or slightly depressed
 With pen I explore and heal, this I confess

A Canvas of Poetry

Do you understand
Why the word poetry does many so offend
Frightens when the power
Of words excite, stimulate and tower
Poetry is not a contagious disease
Quite contrarily, the words soothe and please
Once so engulfed in flow of rhyme
To colonel earth return in prime

Immersed and mesmerized
By language homespun prized
Or slaves to the idiom or sounding phrase
The mind digests to our amazement
Solid spoken, rise to man's greatest gift
Excites us and gives the mind a lift

Some poetry's on higher plateau of our understanding
The philosophic venture never ending
Suddenly the whole world in its beauty now does shine
All poetry belongs to all, by sheer design
In its concocted, screwed-up form, words venture into fruition
No demand, no conclusion, no decision
Word pictures like the myriad of stars shine, illuminate, blink
Touch the very inner soul of mankind in a wordy rink

Just as if subtle, beautiful gifts are absorbed
So similes and metaphors are ever scored
On a giant canvas each phrase so grandiose
Each phrase so meaningful as if to pose
The colors yellow, green, red, blue
To nature and mankind ring true
Each scene a change for we omit the change
A mesmerizing kaleidoscope on unending range

≿ ≿ ≿

Be it the last word or the first word
It's what you say and how you say it that counts

Listen

Be a listener, like me
As I pop off grandiose on
Why global warming will lead to catastrophe
Or excess salt bloats up your body

Or why certain stocks will radiate
While others zoom
Poor soul on other side politely says: "Is that so?"
Loquacious streams of words intoned

My monotone is not enough, ensnares into sleep
I interrupt, pontificate, practice one-upmanship
For I truly know (or think I do)
Took conversation away, listen no more

Learning, observing, my tirade of description
Has long tuned out the other person
Impassioned, driven by some ego, I drone on
While the other anxiously waits for his turn

Forgot what he wanted to say!
So drowned in my own words and thoughts
I am oblivious of what I have done
Did I listen? Hell NO!

And, lonely
I walk off the stage

～～～

*It's easy to have the
last word when you're
the last one in the
room*

275

My Joy of Writing

The joy of writing,
Incessant, so exciting
Words pour out of my heart and mind
Overflowing treasure trove
The sing-song under skin in brain
Each phrase heartfelt again
Of sounds, of words, ideas, many kinds

Writing so real, alive I feel
The story bursts out of its sealed box
Fiction, truth, fact manipulated
Overshadowed much elated
Luscious love and things we hated
All but a page in the panorama of life
So easily contained by gun and knife
Once in print, engrossed and fated
Rhythm and rhyme sing
Poetry strikes a cord
Grandiose vision bring

My feelings
My thoughts
My ideas
My values
My hopes
My loves
My wishes

Spontaneous, cerebral, meaningful
Sometimes confused, incoherent
From the depths of my peculiar brain
Retrieve imprints, distorted memories
All flash by with excitement
Will you share my voyage?
Will you help me interpret the rich flow of language?
And just for a moment - or tomorrow
Share a bit of me - merged into you
You see, that is why I am so grateful
You the reader, curious
Interpreter of life

Power of Words

Wonderful words are simply not enough
Each letter, each vowel, each invitation
Creeps on flowing, weaving sound waves
Audible the letter, the word, the thought
Jumps from end to end

Overwhelming, sounds are silent, smooth
Yet deafening
Crocheted into figments of imagination
Staccato, halting
Rhythmic, emotional
Sometimes sing-song in erratic tune
This supposed language we all speak
What if they all babble Latin?

Words, human breath in a sentence linked
The impending power of each thought
Transmitted and received
Moves more than mountains
Cannot be bought
As the active brain empties out
Words flow physically
So sincere a request

Come read with me
Telegraphed special
Hit the fuming bone
Of curiosity and atonement
Forgive, wish, praise
Is the child's tantrum any clearer
Than a grown ups?

Are you reading aloud? Are you listening?

 ～ ～ ～

The short story was so good, I read it twice
"Like a reflection of myself" I said
Even though I authored it myself...

SIGNS

There are always posts and signs
Notes, scattered
      WATCH YOUR STEP
Dogs On Leash
Dead End!

Meanwhile my mind crammed with imaginary signs
      TURN OFF LIGHT!
      LOCK THE DOOR!
      MAIL THE LETTER!
      RETURN PHONE CALLS!
Flush the toilet!
If that is not enough
There are warning signs
      EAT MORE SALADS!
      BEANS AND AVOCADOS!
      FISH IS HEALTHY!
Less salt!

      GET ENOUGH REST!
No sooner do I step outside
STOP - the sign on the corner STOP - the light
      NO LEFT TURN!
      PAY HERE!

God forbid we miss a sign
      ONE WAY!
      ROAD BLOCKED
      DEER! HOSPITAL!
      MEN AT WORK!

I wonder, like a blind man
In an ancient world;
Will I still find my way?
I like the hotel door sign: DO NOT DISTURB

Corny as hell, but I
      SIGN OFF!

Aren't You The Poet?

"Aren't you the poet?" I was accosted,
Humbly, I am no more a poet than you are.
I felt peculiar - doubtful.
I can't be a real poet.
Have my simple books brainwashed the reader?
Where is the brilliance in language?
Where is the doomsday philosophy?
A poet: What is a poet anyhow?

The poet can conjure words and phrases right,
Rhyming or descriptive
Each language has its poets
But there is a universal commonality;
Poems are about life, about nature
They are the marrow and meat of now
Adulator and critic, charmer and denouncer
Each double-edged phrase
Could be boldly politic, could be savior of suicide
Or colorful description of ... anything

Reinvent the six senses so that you
Cannot only hear, but visualize, inhale and smell
Almost touch the world in pictures and phrases

Pouring out a stream of consciousness

chapter twenty-eight: big spender

Shopping

She says: "Must go shopping"
Reluctant, my eyes are popping

Some neat sweater, slippers too
Or a dozen gifts for a friendly crew

Hit the counter and the sales
Out of her size, she now rails

Kitchen gadgets, saving bank
Gizmos to communicate and crank

See a jacket, shoes that fit
I'm exhausted so "just you wait and sit"

There's some nut in a woman's head
Buy and buy, her mind's direct

Includes the dainty, fancy, circumspect
Full of shopping bags and boxes packed

Special cookies, candies well displayed
After hours I'm dismayed

More store aisles we now roam
Ignored my begging; "Let's go home!"

To each purchase keep receipt
All so tidy, all so neat

Next week's action I have to learn
So many items to return

SALE

"Sale" - sale
Simply to buy
Like mud in your eye
Excitement to shop
Each sale, bargain, never stop
Color, packaging, eye catching, like magic

Fifty percent off, two for one
Entice, advise, shopping is fun
Merchandiser teases, like magnet, every trick
Denying, net coming makes you sick
Check, cash, credit card - or debit; your pick

The price is right, why not decide?
To heck with budget, money between fingers flit
Meanwhile my closets bulge, because I deserve
Excite, exhaust, SHOPPING NUMBS
My every NERVE

More gadgets and electronic stuff
No matter, don't dismay, never enough
Never enough

~ ~ ~

Money, influence and power are comforts
But only while you are still alive

Hooked on Gadgets

Have we fallen so far?
Where is my iPhone?
Where is my iPod?
Must give it a charge
It is my bosom pal
My brain's outlet
A lifeline to my friends, the world
Be it gossip or a stirring cry for help
Let me have my goddam phone!

No, I don't sleep with it in my bed
But after my morning shower
It becomes my daily companion, outlet
So attached that at each buzz, each ring
My impersonal becomes a being
With garbage in
And garbage out
Yes, I admit it   I am an addict

My phone is at the other end of my umbilical cord
It is part of me, alive, latent, waiting to jump, spring
I must look at it frequently
Another message, another answer, revelation
It is a limb, an extension of my body
The insanity of this generation - world-wide
So commanding, so time absorbing
What would I do without it?

Would I go through withdrawal like a drug addict?
Yes, with an undercurrent of craving
Non-existent to the generation before
I guess we all have to spill our brains from time to time
Or every five minutes, now hooked, did I say addict?

Soon there will be new model…
I can hardly wait
Can't you?
My new gadget speaks,

but it doesn't have a heart

≈ ≈ ≈

Why are we all so busy
In a hurry
Going nowhere?

Big Spender

Great pleasure is to write a poem or limerick
And on your tongue will do the trick
You buy your friendship with your spending
Addictive habit of purchases never ending

So, as your purse goes seriously sour
You fret with your depleted cash soon by the hour
For once sucked dry by supposed friend
He turns his back and shows his end

Yet what you buy unnecessarily like a fool
Self-deception mirrors you as you drool
Must use and play with it, must possess
Tragic that this appetite for things does not pass

So many unnecessary goods you do amass
Involved, infatuated, in love with them it's mighty crass
Surrounded by your purchase, kids no one but yourself
You are your own Robin Hood and helper like an elf

Next time in store or catalogue
Object; stop buying like a hog
Will power!
Yes, do let the purchase pass
If you buy, again, show yourself a total ass

My gizmo broke
Serious – no joke
It's kaput, on the blink
I'm speechless, need a stronger drink
I just don't know what to think
Must go in a huddle
And come up with a new model

The Gift of Giving

Too many holiday gifts to buy
Who to skip and who to satisfy?
All those pointless gadgets for the kids
To choose so many turns my wits

      Then there's my fussy cousin
      So critical, I just buy her nothin'
      A dozen friends
      That all depends

Some handy cookware, that's clear
Coupons for eBooks shall appear
The tin box of Belgian cookies
Or lay a bit on the Irish bookies?

      My dearest one, my heavenly honey
      She loves the GELD (I mean the money)
      Best Buy certificates, coupons, cards
      Each gets their own to warm their hearts

And while alert and still in my prime
Good wishes coupled in a rhyme
Gift wrap and name tag is a chore
I give from the heart and then give some more

      In honor of some friends; a charity donation
      Not much appreciated by the youth, so ration
      The giver's heart jumps, full of joy
      In humility, bashful and pretending to be coy

Sometimes I'll receive some nuts or candy
In a shopping bag lug it home so dandy
Best feeling of joy and rip-roaring rife
And hope for another year just to stay alive

Overspend

Bedazzled
Expensive gorgeous blouse
Elegant leather shoes to boot
Dilettante, from most extravagant house
Yet teaser set for romantic mood

Eyes feast on sumptuous gourmet spread
So fancy formal and fastidious
Now fed ruby-red rich expensive cabernet
She gestured, smiled, pressed on insidious

Tickets, seventh row, center in the house
Bid up to pretty buck
Enticing, acting should arouse
Oh Lord, too much to drink – now out of luck

He, elegant siren for a start
She's gorgeous, so inviting
Borrow my credit card
While repartee now so exciting

Romantic movie first
She dared come to my place
Wine now to still the thirst
Must practice self-control, act mighty chaste

Romance and lips victorious
We gyrate, lose ourselves in passion
Our rendezvous so glorious
Soon lovers, bonded in new fashion

She doesn't know my bill's not paid
I'm jovial and full of lust
My dream of beauty close and late
With rapture, love so blind the trust

One day my bills on counter showed
She was shocked, found my bills were tossed
I lived pretentiously under another code
Thus trust, love, and lass I lost

Computer Crashed

The computer crashed
All wisdom, information blank
Electrical storm
All information in the tank
Shock at first
Until repaired, something replaced
Time to think
Time to write
Wiser, enter a new phase

What happened to the back-up?
No more a slave to the computer;
Computer vacation!
No, it's not the end of the world
(Almost though)

New ideas spawn
I recover
So much lost
But so much saved
And it's still functional
My patched-up computer
Give me a pen and paper
An envelope and stamp
Hear my voice on the phone
If possible?

~ ~ ~

We invent so many new things
That our minds just can't comprehend them
Must we have them ALL?

Advertising is so persuasive that we stand in line
for hours to return unwanted

We gabble incessantly on cell phones
But say so little
It's not easy to shut up
Once the floodgates
Are open

The gravitational pull of the internet
drags many of us
into
the
dumps

I used to love children
Now I watch them with their gadgets, I don't exist
I see them but they don't see me

Don't slip under the ladder
While you chase a black cat
It will not cure your superstitions

My car, my gadgets, my clothes
Are all waiting for me and I must buy more!

Gluttony for punishment:
You know I'm too fat.
So why bring cake, cookies, ice cream,
cheese, soft drinks in to the house
Do you want to collect on my will early?

Some of us like to be first in line
And are willing to pay the price in time,
money and effort –
But can we afford it?

A quick fix can turn into an expensive repair

chapter twenty-nine: more flashes of my life

REFLECTIONS

I must save my tears
Haven't I cried enough?
Are the tentacles of life so devious
As to strangle slowly, slovenly
Wearily while the scary soul
And beckoning body is numb
I love this exciting, joyous life
With heavenly bliss comes life's curve

Long life is a great gift
And simultaneously a painful punishment,
Once life was breathed into me, I, the innocent babe
Let me cry, gurgle and smiling, laugh
No warning of the vicissitudes and tests of life!
Let me grow in pleasure some experience
With pain an unnecessary by-product
But now grotesque, one foot in the grave
Disengaging older age
So I synthesize, solidly all past into one momentous memory

Children born
Latched on to wife's career
Emotionally tattered, now rebuilt
Lifetime of medicine
Climbed the honored ladder of success
Denied and saved
Only to lose wealth in
The economic downturn
Helped in the campaign to elect our President
Few good politicians, many devious, lying
Deceitful…

Yet life, love, family, travel:
All passed by so vivid
Like a two-hour
Academy award movie
Life is choice but mostly ordained, destiny
Once shape, born, grafted into a certain soil
Convinced of a learned frame of mind
Right and wrong

We are slaves of our own convictions
And habits
As our body withers
Still the heart beats, the heart beats
In deep pain and in childish raucous hilarity
It still whispers "I love you, life,"
For that, too, is our gift at birth
So I ponder, wonder…

Today is still today, and that counts
As every day is eventful
Until the very last.

I relish

I relish my privacy
My moments, uninterrupted
No TV, phone —ring, buzz
Just let my mind rest
Gray cells in explosive, yet calm explosion

Almost like being confined in a doctor's cubicle
Before the doctor enters
Or the airport waiting for a flight
Walking the cemetery paths after a burial

I relish my privacy
Explore my creative inner self
Realize the precious moment
Mine to pursue, explore

Because it's scarce
Like sunshine
As ideas grow, mushroom
In blazed, dazzling color
A Godly sigh
A feeling to behold

I Crossed the Bridge

In life we bridge many chasms
First effortless, then harder
To the other side
                              Crossing

I was a teacher
Whisked through the demands of education
Filled thousands of young minds with
George Washington, Alexander Hamilton,
The struggle for American independence,
The Revolutionary War
I lived American history
In mind, body and spirit

Yet it was time for change
A new career, aspirations of wealth
I had it all; a wife, Jeff and Judy, a mansion
                              I crossed that bridge

Beautiful Lillian died and
Age crept in, but also new enthusiasm
So here I write, expose and share
No remorse, just enticing tid-bits
My rhymes, my prose, my dreams,
Only the good stuff is yours now too!
I explore my inner self in peace
I crossed that bridge to eternity
                              I crossed that bridge.

☙ ☙ ☙

My mind is made up today
Tomorrow is another story

My Duty

I hug my pillow
As if it was my childhood
Teddy Bear
Secure, to cuddle and comfort
Reminisce about the womb
Close my eyes
In the trance
Of a fairyland

The author and his mother "Mutti" on the
Baltic Sea during an early holiday

Fearful, uncanny, I reflect,
I feel too much pain
Tears hidden in the subconscious, deep
Like oil under ground
Not fractured, about to well
Almost in a comatose state
The aching feeling, I hurt

Those close snuffed out, disappeared
While I in innocence moved
Few anchors, lacked close bond of love
Still dreamed, still hoped
Pursued, glory like foam melted away
Inner strength, survival instinct
An adult long before my time

Devil subconscious
So real, translucent
Reach out and almost touch
The heavenly weight
Confused memory
That child of innocence
Now disturbed and unrehearsed
My best friend's funeral only hours away
Oh, such agony, I'll miss him
No such luck to be born again
Today, no protective warmth
Today; frightful, exposed
I must.

Found ...   and Lost

Lost and found
Looking round and round
If found is never really lost
All that aggravation has its cost

The thought, the search
The stupid feeling in a lurch
Be it glasses, or keys
Utensils, or money that flees

Where did I put it, can't remember why?
Must look, find it, I must try
Often to absolutely no avail
Aggravating loss of time, I still fail

When Nudnick my dog disappeared
The worst I feared
Searched with my car in the neighborhood
Why would she run away? I never understood

"Here Nudnick, here Nudnick" I would shout
Soon the black Lab would appear and pout
A tail slung shyly between her leg
And I so glad to have her back

You know, she was more than a dog who was lost
I wanted her back at any cost
Yes, it can really tear you apart
When you lose a thing so close to your heart

Then, suddenly when least expected,
The gray cells now are reconnected
In drawers, under papers
The disappearing glasses, keys and capers

Have waited for you all this time
While you were searching most sublime
At least I am not as stupid as I earlier felt
Some part of my brain's integrity is still upheld!

∼ ∼ ∼

Memorable ideas of yester-year
Often seem to have no meaning
Other than just being memorable

An Ordinary Wake-Up Morning

Iridescent innocence awakens in half-sensational stupor
The bright sensory shining rays into the brain
The cosmic crashes suddenly upon spinning ideas
Phobias mixed with fables whirl within the half-cocked brain
Eyes slowly open to the gray hushed heavenly morning

Utter silence during the concoction of sound and fury
Just like the bloom of morning flowers open wide
Or the joy to reach the crest of the mountaintop
With wide wonderful vistas.

So too, the congealing pieces of the brain widen
And sort in visual perspectives - "Where am I?"
In a thousand places at once

As the morning light, diffused, beams brighter
So do the thoughts of duties of the day
The menial chores like dress, eating, and toiletries
Soon substituted by grave tiring tasks, stored and incomplete
Waiting for completion

Be they architectural drawings,
Be it toiling on the assembly line,
Be they computer programming,
Harvesting the crops with farm compactors and caterpillar giants,
Voting on a bill at the legislature with serious consequences,
Feeding and teaching the baby...
All are profound in the chain of existence

And all play their pivotal part in the dutiful days' events.
It's still morning before breakfast time,
I have not even parted my priorities into A, B & C.
I have not yet digested the world news at my fingertips
Nor have I given tidy, warm, affectionate greetings
to friends and family.

While my body moves, my arms sway,
Digesting all the reawakening of the morning,

A constant backache reminder of the now
Sometimes I want to shuck it all and call it a day off,
But training and habit overcome this desire for escape.
And we drone on, crawl upward against the current
Subtracting another rich and precious day in the calendar of life.

I Know How I Feel

No hallucinations
Just weird expressions
Bottled up within
Almost irreligious
The loss, the quiet scream
Unspoken agony of pain and loss
So in the gut
The thunderstruck emotion

They say it was a brown
Labrador I say it was the ever-loving lick
The joy when he saw me
The pleasing when I said "Sit!"
Or "Lie !"
Or "Stay!"
The stroke of the warm fur
The sad but caring eyes aimed at me
Always duty bound to retrieve
The loud bark when a stranger came too close

I say the careless driver
Collided with my innocent four legged friend
I grieve
There is an emptiness
I have lost my dear, wonderful friend
I peer at the empty dog dish
No more dog hairs around
There is something missing around here
And only I know how I feel

Collectables

Overwhelmed, overcome
By my own fantasies, seem frozen, numb
Rooms jammed with books, records and pictures
As if I were a scholar of the scriptures

    Statuettes, vases, new heirlooms now in disarray
    Bulging, colorful brown bookcases hold sway
    Boxes full of collectables fill other cracks
    Aged, wonderful wines on racks

Many wine bottles that date back to 1970's
Smooth on the palate if you please
Cabernet, Zinfandel, Petite Syrah, and Merlot
Liquid reds sure worth some dough

    Other considerable cartons full of recording tape
    Tons of boxes full of knick-knacks in many shapes
    No wonder I dare not leave home and travel
    This delightful dilemma first unravel

Grateful to guard my comfort zone
For constant collecting in heaven will atone
Yet my mind is filled with foolish folly
Nuts, too many things, not very jolly

    Some strip naked in hot climates with delight
    Whilst I am immersed, surrounded, feel alright

≈ ≈ ≈

I warned you – I can be wordy
I do not get to the point
which may change during my
rambles and renderings

My Garden

My world: "Up! Get dressed!" my mind orders
Seeds in my dreamy mind conjure, imaginary or real
Time to get ready
Transfixed, I visualize green growth in the garden
Rich green leafy plants, ground mushrooms under trees
Asparagus, ample weedy tomato plants; luscious, juicy
Red strawberries
After weeks of patient waiting, watering, perusing
Sprout up, into nature forms
Transform into various shapes and shades
Not stunted by growth
Mouthwatering, pick and devour
Soon I revert to a mixture of dream and reality
Even the colors of this room
As the sun's rays dance - seem to change
To dull blue with yellow trim as sunlight filters through the beams
Outside, brown dangling octopus-like autumn branches
Stretch everywhere in gargantuan proportion
While before me, the smell of black lacquer from restored shined shoes
And tan gabardine trousers erect with pleats
Quickly stuff keys, wallet, white, neatly folded handkerchief
Into the waiting pockets now bulging
Yet before I leave the room
Not to miss a dash of after-shave
Fragrance wafting, amour with a touch of dare
Can't you smell my after-shave aroma permeating the air?
It's time for breakfast and then some
It's the little changes over millennium
From horse's hoof to three fingers, now five toes
Too many species have already disappeared
Forests denuded, vast orchards
In city, bland and unending suburbs,
While streets and highways sprawl and connect
Our earth's icebergs melt
The ozone layer threatens, but many do not believe
Calamity likes the innocents
The time is not far away
We do not like to drown
Rising sea levels –it will take eons
But few get ready for the rising oceans
Beach dweller where to go?
Rising ocean waves will denude shores
You said little things don't matter
Might as well go out on the town tonight
The garden's been watered

Throw It All Away

How in all this mess
Can I find anything? I have to guess!
Bit by bit I put it there
Hurriedly, piles up as if I didn't care
Too much collected, so easy and addictive
Things to hide behind, protect, most restrictive
Find it, save, and pile it high or low
Best accumulations never show

Extra books, extra clothes, extra fridge
Spread out they easily cover length of a bridge
Rummage sale, auction, stores
Too much that my conscience gores
Where is the room to walk about?
Things take over, what a route
Heavens I better not die
Then all my relatives will cry

Not the end yet, not my demise
It's because there's too much junk for dazzled eyes
Leave behind no inventory
As collector in my glory
Relatives will discard and haul my goods away
Lifetime of collection couldn't stay
Oh what insecurity
To amass what is not purity
Things amassed as a protective shield
Is my burden in the field?

So if you should ever die
Best escape if you can fly
Your monument of meaningless now left behind
While inheritors rant words often unkind
I do forgive you and you do forgive sick me
A lonely, scared and isolated creature that I'd be
Somewhere beyond my grave I'm free
No more junk, no more a slave

chapter thirty: life and death

At the young age of eighty-seven and a half, I sit on the precipice of life and death, leaning much more towards life than the latter. My day is jammed, even with such mundane daily tasks of buying toilet paper, great food and strawberry plants, raising four types of tomatoes and plucking daily a lemon off my tree to zest up my green tea. My week-end calendar overflows with theater, musicals, opera, symphonies, and our famous Speaker's Series of famous personalities, scientists, commentators and politicians on the ascent, even including U.S. Presidents.

Best of all, just had my cataracts removed to give me 20/20 new vision! I still love to drive locally, hire daily helpers, a gardener, cleaning lady, handymen. They all keep me busy and entertained. There are also the satiating, intimate hours with my significant other.

Frugal, my assets grow weekly as do my donations. So you see, if I, or you, had to worry about life and death, the answer is obvious. As long as the mind ticks, as long as we are curious and inquisitive, as long as we have some mobility, and keep busy and interested, why stay shut up in dark black garb and wait for the Reaper? Insane!

Eat well, get a bit of regular exercise and maintain a healthy, alert state of mind; that's all good advice and a prescription for longevity. A sense of humor and a few laughs keep the brain chemicals jumping.

I do have one complaint though. I hate to go to bed. I often do so after one or two A.M. I also hate to get up too early. And when the day comes for me to me to say good bye, I hopefully won't know about it.

Our time on earth is so short, so fleeting. Tell the youngsters: better make the best of it, lest you suddenly find yourself at age 90, full of rich memories that lasted you a lifetime.

IT CAN HAPPEN

It can happen anytime,
Nothing matters - not love
Nor faith, nor hope
The earthquake rumble that destroys all.

Scary shock; "It's cancer, stage 4!"
Homes, family, businesses,
A heap of rubble under which
All are buried in this old Italian town.

I cannot cry, no tears
This is nature, a death knell
Why did I survive?
It is like the slaughter of Gettysburg
In 1863 - few survived
Many maimed
Or the sinking of the Lusitania.

Must we live listen to the testimony
Of all the tragedies that
Fill the pages of history books?
Another Hiroshima - thousands of atomic bombs ready
Global warming: extinct species
Now is the time to act!
Yes, it can happen tomorrow.
Are you ready? NOW!

To some life is all fun and roses until the thorns
take over and nature throws you a curve ball

I Simply Can't

Brilliant, beautiful, translucent
powerful sun's beams penetrate
brighten my atmosphere
a thousand graceful moving shadows
I being one

Only my sour spirit is transformed
into the longing lifeblood of the moment
as if the rays irritated my funny bone
transformed my introverted and idle stance
into a new awakening of brightness

Despite it all, I want to feel good
I want to feel ebullient, robust, happy
I want to taste the full experience
I want to stretch my being beyond the limit
I chuckle, smile, but do not test the impossible

I want to dance to the warbles of bird songs
fly with arms and legs in wild abandonment in the air
free spirited, unchained, uninhibited
I want to strip and dance to the Indian Moon Dance
or barefooted, stomp to the rhythm of free nature

I want to unburden, but I can't!
I want free and open thought, but I am stifled with fear
I want to stay a celebrant but I must shamefully depart
I want to sense the exhilaration of the moment,
but an iron curtain stops me like a turtle

I carry the burden of my personal guilt,
        though I am guiltless

≈ ≈ ≈

*Some rationalize their way to heaven,
others to six feet under*

Threshold of the Universe

With visions and fireworks
Pinnacle on Mount Loneliness
I experience the hues of the rainbow
Frothing, haunting formation of clouds
Cirrus, Nimbus - like angels, scaring demons in the sky
The radiance, the magnificence of life
Uncanny inspiration, all too short!

You and I stand on the threshold of this universe
Confined, deliberate - ready to dare or do
Planted firmly to explore our vision
Open eyed, with little trepidation
Gift of life in all its brilliance
Like Moses holding the tablet of the
Ten Commandments downward - exhorting his people
To abandon the Golden Calf

So you too - here - retreat from the steep mountain
Inspired/halo - visionary
Truth - in awe of The Creator
The Unifier of the Universe

Queen/King of nature's power
Admire, thankful, humble
In this, our place, the infinite universe
The spirit is within you - me!
Yet, we are but on the threshold!

Go, take another first step!

∾ ∾ ∾

Life is like the fizz of Coke
In youth full of bubbles and sparkle
Gradually the taste falls flat and even
And the effervescence dies down

Not Arrived Yet

I have not arrived yet
There is hell to pay
In heaven, not on Earth
So correct in childhood
Attentive, well-behaved
Always in search for purity

Waylaid, mislaid, distracted
Beauty and fun escapes
So many opportunities missed
Matured often too late
Not easy to turn back
Or even find the road

Spy over shoulder - disregarded
Move on - my goal, my day
My pleasure and misfortune
I said, someone knocked on the gates
Of Hell!

Herr devil, too busy
Go back to purgatory and suffer
I don't care about Heaven and Hell
"I'm too busy trying to stay afloat,"
I uttered in sheer despair

The truth, I have not arrived yet.

Spins on Its Axis

As the world revolves
        So too
                Our tumultuous life
Spins on
        Its own axis
              Helplessly
We spin with it
        Barely keeping
              Our balance
Don't you feel it?

Donate Organs

Shall I donate my organs
So another human can see through my eyes?
Kidneys pump,
Liver, gets rid of toxins and God knows what
My heart in someone else's body
My feelings once connected to my brain

Was that destined?
I feel a need to preserve
What kind of person is the receiver?
I will never know

How generous will I be
In another body?
Let's hope the gun
Never fires again
Besides, I'll have an unfinished obituary

Life Train

The heartbeat speeds the rich red blood
From capillaries to arteries
To nourish every nook and cranny
In my sacred body
The instruments, the engine pulls
And off, to travel at increasing speed
Acute, energetic confront the day
Life is not a ball, more a scenic voyage
Not always a sweat-bath
Not an ego competition
Nor an energetic, joyous carnival
But more like a train
Wheels touch the fastened rails
On schedule, making stops
Discarding
And taking in
Heading for a known destination

The engine well lubricated
Two, three delicious meals a day
Joined by crammed fast food stuff
Switched on with heroic speed
We traverse the day
Everywhere the adverts
To tease our hunger

Add a few more cards, a few more pounds
Or fill the room to its optimum point
The tranquil rolling hills
Bridges crossing flowing rivers
And a tunnel or two
With awesome speed
All among nature
Rose fragrances long past
Just a glimpse here and there

And the years whizz by
No chance for a return trip
Moving ever slower on rusty tracks
Maybe to be transplanted somewhere, reminisce
So much promise
So much hope
So much love
Seen so much
Done so much!
Felt so much
See the mementos?

Please let me travel a few
More scenic years
I'll fill them with treasures of golden joy
With you of course!

≈ ≈ ≈

Kooky, crazy, crankily in delirium I awake
I wonder
What kind of day will shape me today?

New Life

From some small atom into a gene
Breath of life in mother's womb
Genuinely hewn, like Adam and Eve
All organs so alert, the miracle
From seed into bloom, blossom, dazzle
We human specimens evolve
Earth break! Earth shake!

Romantic, reproductive spirit
Knowledge and acumen and
Ego and drive
As thought of early youth makes you tremble
Headed into the stratosphere of challenge
As genes tumble actively, excitedly
You bite, salivating on earth's crust

Traveling continents
Aspirations as well as disappointments
Full of passion, love and apprehension
And into the realm of possibilities
With a magic breath of life
A mirror of yourself

So powerful
So precious
So temporary
So fallible and brittle

Life

ᔕ ᔕ ᔕ

Ideas, inventions and fads are fleeting,
as is your life

Being Alive

'Ere I open my eyes, the split lightning sun rays
Sensitive, fuzzy, at first evoke daylight.
Alive for another day?

Maybe? Perceptive, clever, all consuming?

Maybe.

Out of this nirvana state, stare at the sky
Or down deep into the dark abyss not yet surrendered
There are no blasphemous thoughts
No curses yet of what's right or wrong
No deviation from the norm
No quick escape
Into my new, more savory thought process
Just being, being here, and now
So call it "being alive"
And I haven't even gotten out of bed yet!

        But I am exuberant
        I feel happy
        A sunny day to greet me

And maybe, just maybe conscious that I am alive

~ ~ ~

We know but will never admit
That we age until the end,
still unprepared

Lack of sound sleep
Face an ornery, tough day
Cannot escape;
Celebrated earlier
And now it' s time to pay.

Life in the Balance

Not too distant,
The lifejacket tight secure
Abandoned boat, shoes
In trunks.
Ready.

Endless panorama;
Another wet onslaught
Tossed, tilted, turned
Alone - yet I spy land
Thrash and swim, catch my breath
Bob up and down;
So close and yet so far

Waves crest overhead,
The undercurrent deadly
Toward the rim of distant shore
Not drowned yet!
There's energy and hope
Desperately pedaling
Must fight the frigid cold, the elements

Stamina and past practice priceless
Pedaling with all gusto
The resources of God's creature
Come to fight
What timely luck
Of course I'll make it
Yet 30 minutes earlier – life was in the balance.

Some things in life we should not be messing with
Like our death certificates, telling our doctor he's wrong:
Smoking, drugs, overeating
And living a careless, hedonistic life
It's our downfall – digging our own grave
The tragedy of our age

chapter thirty-one: friends

Go, count your true friends. Most of us can count them on one hand. Sure, we have many acquaintances, but true friends are precious and rare. Be it a childhood companion, spouse, or relative, this nurtured, close bond has to be tested, earned and fully trusted many times over. Oh, what luck and joy to have such a wonderful, heavenly association in our lives today. A friendship is more than chatter, spill all, gossip talk. Every friendship is different, yet the cement that holds them all together is similar. It is the magical rapport between one person to another, guiltless and forgiving. It is the extraordinary, helpful, deeply understood knowledge of a true friend, worth more than all the gold in China.

Such fealty and loyalty should come naturally. Having experienced many crises together, maybe having searched and shared much with each other, this mysterious bond grows even closer. Neither side is judgmental but overlooks personal short-comings and faults, relying on understanding and accepting each other's weaknesses.

We express ourselves and exchange opinions freely in front of each other. Similarly, we share weddings, children's births, New Year's parties, maybe even pray or meditate together in one form or another. Friendship is the warm, trusting, open interchange of experiences, fears, events in repartee, answered without bias, prejudice, openly and truthfully, even if mistakes are made. What wouldn't we do for our friends and what wouldn't they do for us?

Often, only after a friend has moved far away or died, do we fully grieve the loss, leaving an empty hole in our being. Yes, we have learned so much from each other, laughed and cried often and openly, without shame, did stupid things and asked for forgiveness, again unashamed. These feelings are so very important. We shower out these unspoken words and often get a receptive, unspoken response, shared and meaningful. These feelings are openly expressed and it seems that, inherently, our friend understands, shows empathy and understanding.

Sometimes our parents and siblings are our best friends, but there is a whole world out there where two people bond over the years outside of the family. That bond is priceless. It has to be nurtured at both ends. I would hate to live in a world without friends, companions, lovers. In my emotional involvement, I wouldn't trade the world for these few remaining friends.

STRANGERS

My neighbor on this street
"Hallo", he's most discreet
Knows little who I am
Deep down probably doesn't give a damn

We seem to live in different spheres
Each to one's own and closer dears
The neighborly attitude of "What's mine is mine
What's theirs is theirs, who cares?" No one will pine

As if an ocean sets us apart
Each throb, each pounding of a distant heart
No neighborly concern of any kind
We, to each other so virtually are blind

Yet when the time comes that one of them should die
No feeling touch, no tears to cry
For by not knowing without ignorance and bliss
What we don't know, we simply do not miss

It's time to mend and keep a chain of brotherly hands
It's time for rational discussions that make sense
In our tolerance and compromise, we practice wisdom's art
And deeply share our world so please don't let it fall apart

New Year Dedication

I like my friends
I really like my friends
Not only for their helping hands
Patient disposition
Their open pleasantries a touch of vision

They are not angry for a fault in me
Or wrong phrase said we should disagree
Their consummate support
No envious jealousy or feelings stored
I like my friends

Their open loyalty and honesty
Their values and integrity
Unselfish support of community
Give time and money with impunity
I really like my friends

When I'm uncertain or afraid
Good counsel from friends
I don't berate
My friends support and call a spade a spade
When I win and celebrate or lose
And simply call it fate

⁓ ⁓ ⁓

I wish most people the best
But for some I have reservations

To be afraid is natural
if you have been once burned, cheated
And betrayed a dozen times

Dismal to Bright

Too short the night
Not right
My choice, stay up to the A.M.
My fuzzy mind into a jam

Ambition, energy did dissipate
Despite the early morn I feel so late
Gray, most forbidden skies do greet
A dismal symptom of defeat

Tenacious, stay awake, decide
Just feel like most abandoned bride
Feel lame, no zest
Hope certainly no one will put me to the test

But then my charming love appears
I fake a smile almost in tears
Adrenaline shot, libido in right place
Her piercing eyes, her charming grace

Thoughtless, I fly into her arms
She frowns, embarrassed in alarms
I kiss her sweetly on her cheek
Does not object, seems quite meek

"So glad you came", I smile
"Please keep me company and stay a while."
Amazing how our body does react
Despite fatigue and much neglect

She sympathizes with my plight
The day awakens and feels so bright

It's OK to laugh alone when no one is looking
But I prefer an audience when I laugh
A spontaneous roar and a good shake

～ ～ ～

My favorite shoes are most comfortable – like certain people that fit me better

313

Special Friends

To say hello - goodbye
Old friend
Kaleidoscope of colors
Each tiny dot a memory
Each color hue an image

Ah, so many talks, walks
Outpourings, happenings
Our brood, our children
Our minds transcend often unspoken
Our human spirit intertwined

Each red, full-bodied wine so strong
Reaching to heaven
To loosen the visionary brain fibers
As we pour out feelings, thoughts
This life a ride with many safe stops
Some shine, some dour, dismal, demanding
With celebrations, confirmations and funerals
Unveiled

Each ash interred into our heart
Part of our human lasting link
And love of man kind
That binds into a proud family
Me and my beautiful Lillian
Patient, pedantic, wise Kurt

Life like a cosmos with
Lives of mopping moon people
Ringing doorbells, extending invitations
Always time to sow and celebrate,
Remember each embrace
For love, life, unity so closely bound

Each day wishes
Barely time to pray
Move into another nest
A constant stream of visitors,
Kids, relatives, friends
Hello - hello – goodbye

Indomitable fantastic friendship
Both ways.

Ember of Passion

The ember into passionate erotic flame
Skip the dialogue, the hasty harangue
Glue your ear to the waves and vibes
Of a melodic maiden
Make the young men swoon
Abandon all, marvelously
Magnetically drawn to her

Who is she?

Scented sensual with perfume
Silk cream skin, open arms
        BECKONING
                With deep tantalizing
                    BROWN EYES
                        Show the world
                            Of lavish love and
            Infatuation

As if in a cocoon fluid
        A BLINDING ring
A magnetic melodic pose
Irresistible - all men drawn to it
Highly hypnotic
Numbs like a hypodermic needle
Some in catatonic, anesthetized state
Some fearlessly fall over the cliff

But I will embrace you and
                Save myself within you
For that eternal moment never
Lasting until I regain full consciousness
Until my heavy
        BREATH abates
And I re-enter the season of reason

                        And sanity

More Than Good Friends

From a distance
A shapely, well-proportioned silhouette
The mind translates and titillates
Stark shock
At close encounter
No it can't be
Weather-worn face, sunken eyelids
Wrinkles at the corner of the mouth
Droopy hanging neck
Eye shadow, makeup, rouge
The dark purple-red lipstick
Enhanced the tragic expression of age
I do recognize her:
"Hallo, how are you?
Haven't seen you in ages."
There was a glimmer glance,
A Mona Lisa smile I could feel love, old times
The spirit yes
Forget the slim,
Well-dressed figure
Oh how I would fantasize her beauty
Our conversation tight, tense, friendly
Anxious voice more creaky yet
There was a shakiness in the vibration
The world's wise, direct and admirable
There was no doubt now, it was she
And yet so long ago
Yes, we were more than good friends.

≈ ≈ ≈

Love bugs, crushes and infatuations come and go,
but friendships bind the spirit and the flesh

Hang around with wholesome productive people
and you'll love longer, happier and it may rub off
on you and add new birth to your own brilliance

Listening is an art
to be constantly practiced
and perfected

I like to brag, pontificate at length
and then I wonder why
my audience disappears so quickly

If your dearest friend betrays you,
Join the crowd,
Get mad,
But hold onto the inner you

This guy I know's a tolerable bore
All eyes on him as he did score

When best
of friends
fight
it's colossal,
It's the
making up
that tests
the mettle

If we both agree
It doesn't make sense
At least we both agree

Be good, if you can't be good, be careful
If you can't be careful, be yourself
The odds are against you
And the consequences you know all too well

I always knew the answer —
But I forgot to tell you
And now it's too late —
Forgive me.

I like people who like me
Well, most of them anyway

Distant neighbors

Got to see each other
Seem fascinating, inquisitive
Exciting, inviting
We met each other
Coming and going
On bus, train, elevator
Coffee counter, church
And grocery store
In rain and sunshine
It is not a coincidence
A "hello", a wink
Not yet a handshake or
How's your kid? Husband? Mother?

It is a rapid, fleeting, human experience
We belong to "them" and they belong to "us"
Yet when we get home into our kitchen
We are one or still part of an extended family
Oblivions in what excitement pain endured next door
Years now neighbors, yet strangers
In neither heart or soul or special feelings

Now most of those wonderful people have vanished
There was life in their glowing, varied faces
The glow turned into a spark, excitement for life
Participated, volunteered, helped
They are almost like ghosts that came and evaporated.
But still like a computer memory
Impregnated into our brain and gray cells
They are my many neighbors, ghosts, and it's my fault too!

Wouldn't it be wonderful if we only took the time
To get to know a few of these folks better as friends, our neighbors?
Are our lives so self-involved, so fleeting?
Tomorrow - maybe tomorrow, a special effort,
I will carefully count the faces and concentrate on them
And maybe, just maybe, with a bit of extra effort get to know one or two
Even invite them over for a cup of tea or coffee or glass of wine

The catch is, will they want to know me?
Does it have to be a crisis, a flood, earthquake, or crime near-by
To bring us together?
Take time out for me, listen and share with me.

chapter thirty-two:
more love and infatuation

Amorous Moments

"You've come a long way, baby!" she vociferously reiterated.
"You listen to me, mostly."
"You read my mind before you kiss and embrace."

Candy and flowers are not my cup of tea, but a splendid dinner with cabernet, elegance, sure ups the ante! Your creative juices… plays, music, theater, concerts, holding hands, dining out.
Most of all the complimentary huzzas before we go out;
"Sweetheart, you look absolutely radiant! What a figure, such fabulous demeanor!"
And boy oh boy, your sensitive kisses, French or not, make my toes tingle! Maybe we should have our own private party tonight, special outfit and all.

Yes, you've come a long way, baby.

The Mind's Path

My mind *matriculates*
Through m a z e s
Conjures, connects
Figures every thought
Sometimes confusing
Other times **pinpoint** exact
Leeches my thought trend
Like a mountain path
It c u r v e s or STRAIGHTENS
But does not deviate
Shows zeal and **purpose**
Lifts my hope and spirit
As indeed I am *challenged*
Effusive, purposeful to
Set up a celebration
With *song*, merriment
And icing on my **cake**
And dance
As we look into each other's *eyes*
In silence exchange
The ritual, the spiritual
A thousand thoughts of ***beauty and love***

Like Vanilla, Rainbow and Citrus Ice-Cream

Anxiety about our upcoming date
Hit it off or end in fate?
How in anticipation will it turn out?
Smooth Casanova or just a rout?
Tension, instant love, or a fight?
Will I, will she, still be all right?

Despicable or euphoric, elated
This special date so highly rated
Outside the calm before the storm
Keep your cool, easy, stay at the norm
After all, it's my choice for this date
I'll be early, not be late
Wonder what am I getting into?
Will I rejoice, regret or rue?

It's the human equation of need
My demanding chemicals to feed
To be close, to share, cuddle
This gathering I mustn't muddle
How will she dress?
Which perfume I can only guess
A man can die from so much anticipation
I wait for her at the appointed station

I see her! I see Her! She's out of this world!
The angels white blossoms on her hurled
Her elegance blows me easily away
"Hallo, how are you," is all I could say
At last receptive, a date or two
A splendid fun-filled rendezvous
It was the sycophantic dance
In close encounter blossomed our romance

Now, years later we are a team
Like vanilla, rainbow and citrus ice cream.

You Marvelous Creature

So many chromosomes, nerve endings
So many sensory organs, perception
All matriculated and calculated in your brain
As the pulse of your ever-beating heart
Refreshes your organs
These precious organs that keep the corpus alive
Resilient, adoptive, perceptive, and resolute
Go, go paint this portrait of your life
Your feelings, your ambitions, your fears
Your hopes and aspirations
What a collage, living, breathing here and now
No artist can fully paint and recreate your magnificent
Livelihood, joy and pain, laughter and happy disposition
That which lies beneath the skin, the taste, the sigh, the sounds
So rich and rewarding are ours; yours and mine to react to
Like a flower opening its petals
Spreading life's beauty and perfume, and so much more
Oh, what great living mystery as you exude,
Brilliantly react to the ever-changing scenes and feelings
As one alive; productive, ever-growing, moving
In gratitude and fulfillment
You, the marvelous malleable human creature
Around you is your life
This well-nourished garden
For the thoughts and deeds you sowed
Many will grow tall and some may perish
But go water, fertilize and enjoy
The temporary blooms in your garden
For life and seasons pass too quickly
Blooms wither and little remains
Enjoy the magnificence, the beauty
Inhale the magic aroma
For you created it

∿ ∿ ∿

No car will ever be as fine-tuned as you.

Her Coy Demands Too Much

Though she's a beauty, anything but tame
A bit airy, stuck up, should I dump her just the same?
So many schemes and material demands
Seem to dominate her present plans
To ridicule, make me a fool
She does it wily, using her most charming magic tool
To her magic potion I succumb
Her charm and beauty make me numb
She's so attractive, leaving is awful hard
How to convince myself it's time to part?
Her penetrating poise and posture mesmerizes
Her charm and compliments beguile, are full of surprises
She gloats delirious that I am her catch
She feels we fit, not realizing we do not match
Must separate, before it's too late
Or be reincarnated bound by an impossible fate
Too late, her personality soon overpowers
Like crushed pea under shoe cowers
In light of beauty I declare defeat
To part peacefully not be neat
But after love potions leave what is left
I, so empty, lost and so bereft
Let me dance and hold you close once more
For beauty in possession I adore

≈ ≈ ≈

Euphoric feelings of love and attachment are healthy, just don't mix dream and reality You may fall off your stool

Creating Love Chemicals

Quiet, Quiet—no demands
Not even holding hands
A realm of inner peace
Soon desire must increase
Love chemicals now cease-please

Nothing, but full, keen mind
Spills over, creates, calculates defined
Active, creative, never left alone
Tries to duplicate or clone
Just spilling, filling, filling

Silencium, yet no vacuum does exist
Portends of plans – love potion to be kissed
Mind's desire
Into action and afire
Where are you? Come closer!

Ebb and flow of hope and fear
Most eventful, hold so dear
Twosome in the privacy now share
Uninhibited show how they care
What a pair! What a pair!

Until from brain to plan to action
Human must find satisfaction
All is a stir of thought
New created what was taught
Like dark clouds before end of the storm

≈ ≈ ≈

A good hearty smile is a worthy communication,
And the reward is if she smiles back

Bathed in Kisses

Awake in middle of the night
Love flushed with blind desire
I find her to my delight
Her tender skin sets me on fire

Ah that enticing perfume, as I arouse
Open her pajama blouse
We kiss passionately in a trance
In close proximity and stance

Half asleep yet close we do adore
Hold fast intense and to the core
Intuitive love flashes overtake
Wrestle lovingly to earn our stake

Several more precious minutes bathed in kisses
Such magic never misses
We gently part to sleep rest of the night
A pair of lovers side by side

Tease & Please

A Mona Lisa smile
Is not my style
Devilish coquette
Never regret
More cheek to cheek
With belly laugh like geek

And if the humor button
Creates loud chuckle not forgotten
So raucous, jovial in her sphere
I see her here, there, and everywhere
My frame and body laugh in pain
It's then I question reason or a touch of the insane

For hormones
Coupled with some testosterone
I woo and chase and moan
My body's prisoner not yet freed
Come lovely one, chance, dance with me

Infatuation

Go, creep under my forehead
And nestle your imprint as I go to bed
Under my scalp the magic, tantalizing buzz
Make thoughts irrational, full of fuzz

Curvaceous beauty, slender
Most exquisite, so tender
A tantalizing, wicked smile
Moves like a gazelle, please stay a while

My testosterone now jumps in celebration
Within me magic joy and much elation
And so you nestle in my thoughts, an apparition
Between what's right and wrong, confused division

I retrieve your awesome imprint and your beauty
Like a computer wants to resolve and keep the booty
Your voice a melody of many tunes
Soothing, cooling, soft reflection of the moons

With compliments and approbation
But more! An energy in syncopation
Electric unspoken— feel this close connection
Wonderful, elated now my inner satisfaction

Of belonging, of attraction and of sharing
Approval, great desire, and of caring
Yet I am so infatuated and almost blind
I never understood what you in me did find

Love Poem

The fruit so rosy ripe
Exceeds last luscious love
As months, seasons, sensations feel rushed
Give us a proper, precious, momentary gift
Includes the tantalizing of the smooth, soft and tender skin
Aroma like perfume into the nostrils permeates the pleasant fragrance
While pungent raspberries tease watering anxious mouth
To top it off, dazzled, almost blinded by her stunning beauty
All senses tantalized conceive a dreamy vision
Love potion tames to tenderness while underneath desire churns
One more kiss, one more dance, one more close embrace
A thousand glances mesmerized by beauty in her face
While mind conjures, computes deep emotions, feelings grow
Enamored full of rapture as the juices flow
Encouraged and enriched, will she reciprocate?
Or will I be disappointed and much agony now my fate?
"Open your lips, whisper, and tell me how you feel."
I stand in awe for I know that our chemistry is real
Take one step closer and reveal my inner urge
And pray that passion and our feelings soon will merge
As in a dream of lovers first foolish most exciting pact
Grows into vivid romance played out in our second act.

Golden Gate sunset, San Francisco, CA

I can hardly wait

I miss you
So kiss me, kiss me
Tongue to tongue tease
As you please
Don't ever stop
Embrace and pop
Thrashing, most refreshing
Sensuous embrace
Massage my back
Another juicy peck
Feel heavy breath
Eternity is now
Kiss forehead above my brow
So kiss me
Miss me
Please don't bait
I can hardly wait

327

Love Binds

The song of love so painful pines
Youth infatuation of all kinds
Until the right one comes along
Know in heart and soul where you belong

So spirited, sensational entwined
With wedding rings you two soon bind
Top off a honeymoon, excited
So dearly heart and soul invited

Adjust to foresight, hopeful dreams
Life's endless opportunities it seems
No two people could be more proud
And constantly affirm their love aloud

Throughout, sealed is their love and affirmation
The tie and bond, feelings of elation
The simple gifts showered on each other
As lovers, friends like any brother

In sickness or wellbeing each at the other's side
Their love, affection reverts as groom and bride
Favors, deep feelings and concern
In heart and spirit earn and learn

If lucky into old age this love persists
Overcomes all tragedies in their midst
Both past and future, retain a bit of youth
So nurtured, caring, pleasant to soothe

From the whirlwind of early romance
Life in rhyme, a melodious dance
The tempos like the foxtrot step
Gold stars all over the biography map
For each so loyal, true to each
Neither one will cause a breach
For love and life victorious do appreciate
For happiness and sorrow may be their fate

Lapping Up Your Tale

Too late
No brainteasers please
Just talk
Talk your guts out
Show anger, disappointment
Or romantic intercourse
Step by anticipated step
Let me lick up every exciting phrase
Let me travel with you in your dream!
Want to leave me?
Want to run away?
"Good riddance."
Where to –
Another city, countryside?
Without pity
Let me know when you find yourself
I'll be there again
Lapping up your tale.

᠃ ᠃ ᠃

If Love

If love suddenly *lands in your lap*
Cuddle it
Cater to it
Cajole it
Cradle it

Guard it wisely

chapter thirty-three: let the world in

Unshackled

Once in a while, mystic, powerful emotion envelops all, consumes us, as if in a crazy, irrational, happy sphere. Unbounded, free we feel fully internally liberated, if only for moments.

Our spirits, thoughts and hopes ascend upwards, like gas lifts into the upper atmosphere, all chains broken. Strut free and unencumbered – let loose! Extemporaneously live with joy and expectations, so blindingly positive it hurts. All aspects of feelings gravitate taste, love, music, touch, with colorful clinging visions to denounce one as a creative lunatic.

It's OK to touch heaven to envision the almost perfect, to parade securely among all mankind, an apparition of a benevolent potentate. I salute you world.

I May Find Myself Again

Some of us never get used
To the tedious routine of every day
When pushed by daily chores, or job
You toil, escape duty, work some more
Some love their job, the bakers, doctors, CPA's
Devoted teachers instill, share and spark
Vie between a guilt complex and escape
Makes me belligerent and mighty sore
Today I want to goof off
Yes, break the chains - one day,
Just one special day
One day only - spirited, hopeful
My day - my freedom day
Rest, read, sleep, goof off
Recharge the battery
No bother, no pressure, no phone
No ring at the door
No computer screen
Just me and my thoughts,
An eerie contemplation of the now

To eye and eye
To like what I see
To know what I can be
To investigate the real me
Forge into myself in a benign way
Discard bad, let good vibes stay
To relax in what I do
Try to myself be true
To weigh myself in this complex world
Peek deep into my sacred soul
To heal, make parts whole
And someday,
Maybe someday,
A little action
A little more satisfaction
And I may even find myself again

Two worlds apart

That morbid, bearded creature
Wretched, wrought by alcohol and drugs
Sad, sorry, saved but for another day
In a cramped, dark sidewalk entrance
Perusing, peeks at me
Me, solid, sober, walking with purpose
Waylaid by this human adversity

It is as if he were in a cage looking at the eager visitors
Or maybe I am in the cage looking at the free-spirited
Waiting to talk, grimace, perform
No, I am no ordinary ogre
I give the man a green bank note
Here we are; I stand, bent over
He reposed, gasping, leaning against the cold stucco wall
There is silence as he stretches his
Arm to take my dollar
Two worlds apart, yet momentarily so close

Open eyes

There is beauty everywhere
Open eyes, see that we care
Canvas of green and grays silhouette
A colorful, candid blanket never to forget

  Varied terrain covers the hilly landscape
  Or denuded forest from a rape of man
  There is flora and fauna and a brook
  Birds, bees, butterflies if you just look

Not every nature scene is clean
Sometimes decay and waste obscene
There is stench and ugliness in places
We frown with pessimistic faces

  Unseemly, degrading, awesome views
  But in spring and autumn buds good news
  Mesh beauty and ugliness with one view
  Alive, in being all we see is true

We all breathe and live on this sacred soil
While beneath are rich mineral and oil
It's what we see, and how we see it
Jubilant, partake a bit, partake a bit

  Energetic shout and rave and rant
  Help change, most tolerant
  We are the creators, the doers in our time
  Open minds, open eyes, still in our prime

The gray-haired, the bent over, or the toddler in balance
Or the violinist, gymnast taking a chance
Marvel at immensity of the sky, the Milky Way
The vast panorama we view each day

  Sometimes we need a new perspective
  Or keen eyed detective
  For nothing is ever the same
  It's as if nature plays its twenty-four hour game

Bombarded with sensations each minute, each day
These are our lifeblood and they won't go away
So call yourself lucky and ever rejoice
For in life full of action we are but moveable happy toys

Ego Trip

In my innocence I did not know
How to bend, to kowtow or to bow
Wide open, sharp, the echo on my auditory lip
I confess I was on a challenging   ego trip

As lion self-pronounced as king
Herd all the lionesses into a roaring ring
To hunt and dominate and roar and flip
For this great creature was on an   ego trip

So I too must win that game
Hit home run proudly, just the same
King of the hill to mountain tip
Innocent, yet on my   ego trip

Enamored, latched onto this beauty
Cemented friendship as my booty
In the courtship I outdid
Oblivious in venture, on my   ego trip

Later, in philosophic gesture I did write
A critique of the past now well out of sight
And wisdom pearls out of brain did drip
Prisoner, passenger on an   ego trip

And after family and all my friends
For failures and mistakes we did make amends
Vacations wide would never skip
Aging voyager remembering my   ego trip

When then the mirror so reflected
All the dreams and goodies I selected
By this time all my friends would quip
Go forth and complete your   ego trip

Opportunity

9:15 AM - The doors open up ahead
    All fortune favors fortitude
        It's yours to earn, take what you can get

An opportunity in lifetime's interlude
    Go to it, don't be a prude
        But if restrained and prisoner of soul,

Disheartened, disillusioned so within,
    Rebirth yourself, once again be whole
        To lose this lovely day and time would be a sin

Hold on to this tailspin you are in
    The gates of opportunity wide open
        It's yours, so, cowboy, do some roping

Rare, few opportunities await
    Most so inactive
        Realize only when it is too late

≈ ≈ ≈

Barely can wait...

Recent compliment to my 87 year old self
"I envy you and I wonder
How you managed to live so long?"

Enjoy a good meal, be agile, exercise
Have real sex and smile – never force it

Barely can wait for tomorrow!

You've Got It!

Talent to spare
Talent to care
To demonstrate
Or new shape create

      You've got it!

Oh, I envy such creatures
Who display gifted features
Be they athletes, artists or scientists
We adore, cherish them

      You've got it!

Geniuses produce new medicine
Invent tools to keep our air and water clean
Compose new musical tune
Make the young maidens swoon

      You've got it!

Or demonstrate Olympic fate
Open new venues, opportunity's gate
On pedestals these greater leaders
Greatest authors for us readers

      You've got it!

Witness great philosophers explain or warn
Geneticists invent new grains and corn
And yet all of us have talents too
We shape tomorrow's society, me and you

      You've got it!

No rioting, no fuss
There is a gift and talent in all of us
Go, climb the ladder to your success
It takes diligence, hard work to truly confess

      You've got it!

Possibilities

You know, the world isn't all
That it's cracked up to be
Yet lurking in the shadow are your possibilities!
A world of opportunities for all time
How dare risk take on the new?
An infinite universe of possibilities
If you call putting a triangle
Into a square hole
Concentration!

Possibilities

It all depends on the open door
Who walks through it
And what did they do
With the hole in the doughnut?
Life is an exciting constant puzzle
Don't despair, you'll make it

Possibilities

Yes, most reach our plateau at age forty-fifty
Complacent, tired, somewhat satisfied
So much is just pleasant
Why bother?
And yet a surge, a spirit of youth can return
Dare test your inner strength
Change, experiment, risk!

It's yours - the package of possibilities
– waiting!
Love, life and what are you going to do about it?

Possibilities

Let The World In

Open the window, let the world in
Share   inhale
See the moonlight beams
                    create shadows in your eyes

Hear rustling leaves, in a forest most supreme
But out in space things are not always what they seem
New sounds   smells without delay
                    Watch dust dance on an unlit beam

Cold air, warm air, fresh and awake
Hustle   bustle
Gather your things, your soul
                    Leave, get outdoors for goodness' sake

With joy I share my inner heart
My longing feelings will not part
With you, for hand in hand
                    We confront nature's stirring element

What if it rains or snow comes inside?
What if grey dust permeates the air?
Just close the window
                    Let the world bounce off the window pane

≋ ≋ ≋

Inject creative energy and bypass the stars to infinity

≋ ≋ ≋

The doers of the world are the movers and shakers
Mostly earned, self chosen
Big egos and dominant personalities
The good ones are the heroes of tomorrow
And then there is Me and You

Ecstatic Energy

Restless, bag of anxiety

Go kill time outdoors
Pure light blue sky tinged with white
Announces spring - this warm bright day
      Excites the mind
           Nerves titillating
               My doing!
Feeling the rebirth
Of freshmen and romance

Testosterone under the skin explodes
Sizzling to jump out of your body
The mind bombarded by sparks
Ringing the bells of bright visions
      Hormones too tumultuous
           The afternoon sun bears heroically
               On this special day of firsts

All I wanted was a book from the library
But I got a songful of happy beams
To last me through the afternoon
You may call it a waste of time
      To me, it was another celebration of the season
           Sometimes the most simple is the best;
               Time and nature do the rest

LOVE THE WORLD

I treat myself
For whom else would
Or should or could?
And after a day of hard labor
Celebrate, cooperate with friends
And spring, and sing
As if a celebration of a king
So soothed, self-satisfied
Shine in self-glory, knowing that I have tried
If much else is missing,
That's alright;
Free spirit tempered, that's me
Seek honey for the nest like a honey bee
For I love the world, myself and me
Know what I was, am, and soon will be

Thoughts into Deeds

Say what you think
Think what you say
Suspicious eye and ear
Beware, the two-sided sword, the word
A bit more tact and caution
Will open doors
Keep decent scores
Mark of truth in sound
In repartee all around
No recrimination
Our thoughts our own
And if perchance we disagree
Or opposites collide
They are but messages and warnings
Could soon turn into deeds
It's your call
Make sure it's not your downfall!

Human beings
communicate
with sophistication
But do we need all
the garbage
and so little
substance?

chapter thirty-four: dance, dance and other fun

Dancing and other fun!

Once upon a time, eons ago, in the Covent Garden Opera House, London, 3,000 of us danced to our hearts' delight. I, a young teenage American soldier in a sardine can, enjoyed listening to the 30 or 40-piece band, but was a novice dancer. Every third set the 2,000 or so women had their choice to cut in. I was thankful for the shortage of men on the floor, where opera seats used to be. Of course, ever so often, a slow set would warm the heart with hugs and heavy breathing, often not reciprocated in my case, but very alluring and enticing. Besides Covent Garden, there were 1000's of dancers nightly also in Hammersmith during the blackout and Buzzbomb strikes of 1944, and it was well worth the Tube ride to get there.

Once I returned to the States, I graduated from the Aragon Ballroom in Chicago to other ballrooms in Toledo, Cleveland and Indianapolis and other cities, experiencing the mystique of music, partner connection (which I usually found by 10 o'clock, when most dancers "coupled up"). I worked diligently to find a dance partner for the evening, but, basically shy, I usually ended up single in my room. It was the time of Ginger Rogers and Fred Astaire.

Later in life, on my seven world cruises to the Mediterranean and Central America, Lillian, my wife, and I usually closed the dance floor with energy and zest, making many friends clap, and reaping compliments. Our vibrant and active dance routines helped cement our 44 years of marriage. Lillian was a fabulous, instinctive dance partner. There is a certain exuberance as unconscious mind, music and mood come together in a frenzy (or smooth flow) which goes beyond holding hands, coupling up; more of a melding of mind and music.   *Barnum and Bailey Circus*

Dance Uninhibited

Within this marvelous, miraculous space
  On sound footing, if only temporarily
    Dolled up and dancing deliriously
      Abandon all pretenses
      So lavish, liberated, unlimited
Unleashing a spasm of total freedom
  Steps devious, unplanned, circular movements
    Flaying arms, uninhibited body contortion
      As in an African love dance
      So meshed with heart, mind, body
      So fabulously free to gyrate
Twirl, step, rhythm often disjointed
  Movements full of sheer joy, euphoria
    Like the smiling crawling babe ogling nearby toys
      A cheerful teenager mimicking a favorite song
      All wrapped compulsively within the moment
      As if heaven and earth fused in love
To occupy the overflowing, emotional experience
  It is the dance of life, of living
    Of one moment into the next
      Oblivious of an iron-clad, demanding world
      But not here, not now
      Roaring, raucous, radical, revolutionary
Or gliding smoothly like swans
  Without restraints, without limitations
    Without restrictions nor reprimands
      Just to be witnessed
      In this tiny space, somewhere on earth
      In an aura of innocence
The human expression as it unleashes animal spirits
  Suddenly liberated to its very roots
    If only for a moment without judgment
      Without censure or opinion
      As even the Gods smile down
      Envious of the sight

Invitation to Dance

"Would you like to dance?"
   First slow - *one two, one two*
Test, touch, tease
   The toe, ball of the foot
Invite as puppets on the dance floor
   An invitation to dream
To breeze and fly
   In whirling movement
Revolve waltz
   A *one-two-three*
All with gusto, rhythm
   Come, watch
The rhythm beat
   Once - *twice, repeat*
From foot to leg
   So gently float
Like a heartbeat
   One - *two* I know you
Entwined with me
   But what's your name?
A pair in step
   Do glide, hop the polka
Supreme twist and turn
   One - two, one - two
Three - four, ever more
   Now hear the drum
The cymbal beat
   Beat, beat, join in
The saxophone, guitar
   Love's rhythm dance
Our hormones' vibes
   Glisten in our eyes
Turned on - turned on
   One - two, one - two
Always the beat - always the beat
   Music naturally absorbed
Forward, backward, circle round

Step - step,
  Step - step
All submit to the master's tune
  Our bodies bend and blend
Like lulling, repeating waves
  In unison, step
The beat, the move, turn
  "Good songs - yes?"
Another gentle turn
  Now more succinct
Now more distinct
  Couples rejoice, graceful
Some getting bolder
  Athletic prowess
Ra-ta-ta, ra-ta-ta
  One-two, one-two
Listen, listen
  Watch, watch
Bedazzled, amazed
  The rhythm of the human race
The feel, the feet
  Totally immersed
Adventurous beat
  Always the beat, second nature
And dancing feet again
  Alas, alas
The music slows
  So sexy, sensual
Only the dancer knows
  Slower, *dip, dip*
And up, tip, top, turn
  Reserve a delicate distance
Warm, gentle hands
  Desire, yearn
Desire - not evident
  The dance of dances
  Ends

A Date

Wrong way, long delay
Exasperated lag, unexpected drag
Can't I get there?
Can't stop, fret there
So I shout out loud without my gag

Complicated, so frustrating
This game of dating
The terms unpleasant, to say the least
Brought her candy, brought her flowers
My anxiety increased by the minute, by the hours

Will I meet her, will I greet her
Set a seat so close to purr
Hold her right hand, hold her left hand
Will she like me, let me, understand?
Yes to woo, careful not to overdo!

Will I suit her?
She's much cuter
Touch her arm, touch her finger
Will she stay or only linger?
Vibes correct, how will she react?

Our first session, first impression
Smiles and gives me the eye
I reciprocate and almost die
A bit cheery, don't be leery
Tease and please her
Big hug hold her
"Not there!"
Like a bear

As I pine, we do entwine
Right vibration, good sensation
Getting late! What a date!
Will it last? Has it passed?
What a blast!

The Troubadour

In deep magician's slumber I rest
Phased, am now recharged at my best
I share with gremlins and the Lilliputians too
A state of metamorphic green and blue
I am no monster, jester, caricature or clown
I inhale, spew, grimace, even frown

And greet YOU as odd and demented
With huzzahs and word bullets long cemented
I am a nonsense troubadour
A throwback to the days of yore
A sheer destroyer of common sense
With metaphors and similes so dense

I play, bark, harangue and shout
I tell a story to an eager crowd dispelling doubt
Sometimes acerbic, bitter but true
For in reflection it may be you
Yet if I go on I'll break into pieces
This dialogue of nonsense and hot air never ceases

≈ ≈ ≈

After-age mating
After-age dating
Is a piece of cake
And gives us white hairs.

Momentary Dance Party

All that razzmatazz
Sounds, beats, tempo
Incessant gyrations
Tempo, music, body in motion
The mind beats to the tune
The rhythm of the body

Free spirit dance, not lost in transition
Like the Hottentots
Indian war dance
Hawaiian wedding bells
Dance, shake, rock, waddle
Rotate head
Careful, lest it twist off
Vibrations, elations

Jocular smiles, shrieks of joy
Celebration of the moment
Inside, within, spiritual
Each song, each dance
Its own meaning
It's all that razzmatazz
Each dance within confines of culture
Movements personal yet universal
Momentary vibrant dance party

Suddenly
Outside the walls - guns blast
Insane terrorists
The world goes crazy
Body parts and all
Inside this nightclub in the Middle East
A shattered world

Running late?
Should I go anyhow?
Late again
Upholding my reputation.

Some walk or dance or jive
Rhythm in step to stay alive
Heart, mind all in tune
But the party ends all too soon

We danced late into the night – a peck on the cheek
The memory of more is mind-consuming

It's exciting to wait for a first date
Will imagination exceed reality?'

If I annoy, you can dump me
Walk away, ignore, leave and lump me
But if I you please
You can give me your keys

If you want to impress someone,
stay young at heart and listen up

Sparks, NV fair

Often we open our mouth too soon
and shut it far too late

Some people have good profiles
Others look better from the back

The mountains are full of precious stones –
but few of us know where to dig,
and even when we find a good one,
she may still need to be polished

To love with all your heart and soul
Assumes you have a soul

If you can't find a reliable spouse
At least get a decent dog or cat to stay –
care for the living.

They say hate and love come out of the same
basket,
Both exert energy
We must quench hate
Love will take care of itself.

chapter thirty-five: believe and give thanks

Thanksgiving Prayer

I bend my head in prayer

Thanks to kind men and empathy.
Give thanks for magnificent sound and music.
Thanks to my triumphs, let my failures be healed
It is through trial and error that I perceive.
Recharge for new adventures.
Charge my language with caution and truth.
Defy falsehood and evil.
Let me partake in the feast of Thanksgiving
For me, for my family, friends, and all mankind.

Let me be patient with those who insult me.
Open my heart to learning and love of life.
Let goodness exude into action
Let my mind be stirring-see all the colors of the rainbow.
When I feel lonely, forsaken,
Let me recharge anew to feast on the joys of life.

Let me be charitable and merciful.
Squash destructive thoughts.
Temper my feelings for wrongdoers and enemies.
Let them see the light if they cannot see their way
Let me find my way to my inner self
Though imperfect, I am good; I form and create.
I wish success, and nourishing learning.
Infuse a heavenly truth and kindness.

A Bit of Quiet

Sometimes

In this tumultuous time
    A bit of quiet,
        Silence,
            Is just fine
                No radio,
                Stereo, iPhone
                Computer
                    Or TV

Just
    I   on   I
        A world of me
            And as you sit,
                Silently contemplating
                An endless world of ideas
                    Picture the real you within

Soul   and   heart
    Sit
        Like Buddha
            On a space of nothing
            Soon,
                Your eyes closed,
                  But your mind alert

You may
    Relive
        The best of your past
        Or perhaps
            The best
                Of your future

Good Intentions

On this day
In my way
Did I help the poor
Did I take time to listen
Did I improve the world one iota more
Did I love and share love
Did I uplift or was I uplifted
My human touch to those so gifted
Did I study, read, learn
Lose my inhibitions, hope and yearn
Did I tell you I love you
Did I repay my bets or debts

Oh wondrous day
Before I fall asleep
Wish me, protect me
Good intentions I must keep

≈ ≈ ≈

To reach out to your
fellow man
is not always
appreciated;
rejection hurts

But if the advance is
fully accepted;
a feeling so grateful and
godly;
The effects last a life-
time

You Are Not God

After a long rest
Giant man is free
Chain untied
World ready, right

There is a storm about to brew
Man's joy of life, of love
Now rejuvenated anew
About to consume and succeed

Unfathomable strength, impossible feat
Creative genius nurtured with amazing zest
The world so infinitely beautiful and yet grotesque
In arrogance I want to rectify

Or put my earthen stamp
Move the mountain
Change the world
Huge colossus, your turn to shoot

Victorious now, or aborted
Yet one bit of advice
I'll say it thrice

You are not God
You are not God
You are not God

≈ ≈ ≈

Much of what I have said, written and thought
I would like to erase,
But like time, all is in the ether of the past,
in cyberspace
And the damage has been long forgiven

The Gods, Nature and You

You who are mighty, so profound
Command creators

Bathe broadly in your elevated ego
Scepter over your firm realm

Adulated, adored, admired
Frown, feared, fortunate

But you are older
And I am not

and

I wouldn't trade
In my beautiful
and
blissful abode
A touch of faithful fear

For none of us is omnipotent
Nor king of his hill forever

Though we may soar like eagles today
We are irresponsible, lost, ignominious in a typhoon

Soon to disappear

And be never heard of again
Nor any memorial of our great life
      Though short and sweet

But I am here today in awe
Of noble mother nature's beauty to behold

and

Lick and lap each mangy morsel
Each aroma, every melodic tone

To absorb and behold
Mine in my brain, my being and my person
Magnificent and magic, so momentous

    This very moment.

        Can't you feel it too?

You know the end will come
So on your way, make of life the best
Nature soon will take care of the rest

Still Alive

Fantastic—still alive
"Yes I am"
"Heart attack."
Yes.
Artery closed 98 percent
Emergency procedure
45 minutes new angioplasty
Open the artery, clean
Plug the hole in the groin
Where the wire went
New type of plug
Send you home tomorrow
New strength, new air
No heavy breathing
No extreme fatigue
You're OK
On borrowed time, of course
But, then, aren't we all
On borrowed time?

～～～

*Man can try to imitate God —
but please leave me out of it.*

If someone out of kindness offers you a hand
Hold it gratefully in yours

Body and Soul

It is not
How
Tall
A man is
Or how muscular and strong

It is what he does
With his knowledge
His dignity, compassion
His place within family
and community
That counts

His use of god-given talents
Is how
His time on earth is measured
Hewn gravestone's inscriptions
Don't do full justice

Two of Arthur's grandchildren

Remember - all our souls
Touch the same earth
And eventually rest in peace
Transformed into dust and skeletons
Soon forgotten

≈ ≈ ≈

*The train conductor knows how
to operate the train
But do his passengers know
where they are going?*

*Saints Peter and Paul catholic church, North
Beach, San Francsico, CA*

I Resign! To You I'll Leave It All!

I feel the spirit, feel the call
No time, must escape despite the mess
Away, away from all I possess
Let me like monk or wise hermit feel free
The light, at end of tunnel see
I yearn, I search
Forlorn, I am in a lurch

In deep prayer, much contemplation
I search for answers with elation
The infinite awe I sense
My inner being – most immense
But truly I cannot now escape
I am complex, I'm not an ape
Secluded, safe, a voyager in a distant place
My foolish follies I must erase

Are these not thoughts and apparitions?
So turbulent in brain with indecision
Is it possible to leave my things, to break loose?
A new adventure and environment I choose
Part with dear friends and family
Start over clear and free
Or leave this world and die
No deal. I simply leave – away and try

I look forward to rest and sleep
But I hate to leave the day unhappy
So what's a happy thought at bedtime?
The peace and serenity of
Forgotten dessert, recall, joyous day of youth
The quiet beckoning night
Come my love – peace, quiet, tranquility
All is right – Good night

Stick Around

Was this day to be my very last?
        Excited visions of my past
                Same love, same excitement I would favor
                        A radical, rich, raving life of flavor

Were this end of day my very last
        I proudly laud the many roles I cast
                From life and nature in the great outdoors
                        To sensual, serious mating on the soaring shores

Not all was perfect, and I do regret
        All the beautiful people I never met
                No medals, genius, or excessive rewards
                        Just hard work, belief in average cards

In my way I spread great values to my kids
        Keep a sane balance in their midst
                Show goodwill, try to be kind
                        In little things of love and pleasure find

To fight the devil when least opportune
        With heavenly, loyal love in midnight's swoon
                Once cast in youth to do my very best
                        In pursuit of happiness I think I passed the test

So do I thank you, loyal friends
        Whose hearts I do accept with open hands
                Whose laughter and whose sadness we all shared
                        And found that we belonged, and that we cared

So thank you God and nature, all
        I rest my case, am waiting for the call
                But then again, with a Mona Lisa smile
                        I'd really like to stick around for quite a while

≈ ≈ ≈

If it is not doomsday
Let's celebrate 'LIFEday'
Here's to you.

chapter thirty-six: biography

When I was twelve years old, my mother, Mutti, turned me over to the American "Kindertransport" which helped about 1,200 – 1,400 Jewish children escape Germany at the outset of the war, without their parents. I then spent my formative years with various foster families in Chicago. From '43 to '46 I served in the US Army, and from the fall of '44 to early '46 I was stationed first in London to clean up damage during the V1 and V2 "Buzzbomb" raids, and then in France and Belgium as a member of the Combat Engineers, feeding over 10 million people. Later, I acted as an interpreter for the US for the 400,000 German prisoners of war.

After the War ended, I earned my B.A. in History and Political Science from Roosevelt University and an M.A. in History from De Paul University. I finished my Ph.D work (but not my thesis) at the University of California, Berkeley. I later taught History and German in public schools for twenty-seven years.

I am that Child

A flashback, I see
That skinny 12 year old me
Same stirring brain
Same piercing eyes
With the ghosts of yesterday inside
Refuting gore and the lies

My ears hear the haunting cry
The mocking sound
Ridiculing, defaming, despising me -
"Jude, Jude!"
Fearful I - move on and defy
Red, black and white the Swastika
Der Sturmer, demeaning caricature
Hooked nose with damning epithets
Heil - Heil -
A giant wall-paper pattern of raised arms
The machine of clicking heels, brown shirt and SS
Wenn du nur eine Mutter hast, so danke Gott
Und sei zufrieden!

Thank God if you still have a mother,
Thank God and be satisfied.

At twelve I was shipped on an eight day passage
Safe now in the U.S
News of the terrible Kristallnacht
The night they burned hundreds of temples
Arrested and beat thousands of innocent Jews.
Mutti and my aunts experienced this incomprehensible terror
Neighboring youth, on order, came into the house

In a few moments, all three stories
Pieces of furniture, crystal, dishes
The store, the windows
The stench of defecation Mattresses cut,
Bed sheets torn,
No one and nothing could stop them

My uncle beaten yet innocent
Was sent to a prison cell
Grandma Omi to Auschwitz
And her son Karl to notorious Gurs, France
Died in the ashes
He proved his German loyalty in World War I
Wounded and received the German Iron Cross
But now crosses and scars
Did not matter

Of my mother's family
Only she and I survive.
Myself a small piece of life - saved
Unlike the other one and a half
million children
I am alive, here, an American, a
solid citizen
After a voyage of solitary struggle
Helpless against the suffering of
my family
An ocean away.

I love this world.

I am that child.

Little Arty at 10 months

My Bedroom

My bedroom at 9 Minister Stueve Strasse, Hanover, was mine, and only mine. It was a separate room, narrow, with a commode and a hideaway bed that lifted against the wall in the morning to allow for more play room. There was a wardrobe for my clothes (there were no closets in Germany) and several bookstands for my books, a chair and a small desk.

Most importantly, there was a three or four foot-high puppet theater which could fold outward, with a pullable curtain. Next to it, a box of some thirty-five puppets, small enough for my tiny hands to maneuver inside the characters' heads , while I enacted an imaginary story. There was a larger King, crowned of course, as was his wife, the Queen, and many plain serfs or "Burghers". Most precious to me was the crocodile, though. The stage was eight or ten inches deep, with a sketch of woods and houses, all drawn colorfully by me, untalented, but still affective. I would change the background from time to time.

Often, in a daydream, I visualized, like other young children. I'd stare out of the large window that faced an intersection of several streets, with a view further off of a large city wall and a steaming heating plant. I spent hours looking out of that window wondering, thinking, day-dreaming. Somewhere in my room we kept a small suitcase packed with emergency clothes and a single book. No-one told me of its existence till later, but it was there for years, just in case of a hasty departure.

This must have been around 1935 at the advent of the Storm Troopers marching outside that same window.

My Father goes into Hiding

Every Saturday and Sunday, I would overhear my mother and her friends talking about the Nazis garroting and choking the Jewish economy. I was pulled out of our public school because I was Jewish, forced to go to a newly-established Jewish school downtown in an old Jewish community center, with outstanding Jewish teachers who also had been removed from their posts, as had judges, lawyers and doctors.

Even my dad, a successful travelling grain salesman with a chauffeur, had to now use a bicycle to visit farm cooperatives. When two of his non-Jewish friends were arrested because they collaborated, he silently went underground. He slept at various friends' homes. When the Gestapo came looking, he simply was not home. Once, my mother was heavily interrogated at the police headquarters, but in total innocence, she did not know where Dad was hiding.

1929 Art and Mother
East Prussia

The Auction

Things came to a head, when, one day at the age of ten, Mutti took me to our best family friends' apartment. Uncle Arnold and Tante Adele had lost their son in World War I and received a meager pension. In their clean, small, two bedroom apartment, we were always welcome. They had an enclosed porch which soon became my temporary home and bedroom.

Mother was gone all that day. When she returned with only a few bags, she announced, "Everything is gone. I had to auction it all off."

In one single day, almost all of my toys, belongings, our piano, oriental rugs, paintings, kitchen utensils, our extensive library, everything, went under the auction hammer, I was told. She handed me four of my precious puppets; the King, the Queen, the crocodile and one single pawn, but not the theater itself. She also saved James Fenimore Cooper's book, "Leatherstocking Tales" in German and a copy of Rudyard Kipling's "The Jungle Book". I still have one of them. I don't remember what happened to that small hidden suitcase.

Forgiving is easy
Forgetting is nearly impossible

I don't know when my end will come
That's why I am not in a rush

Almost Holocaust

No number burned into my arm
Just all around the inside
                    Of my skull

Reflected in
precious grey matter
Easily retrieved

So alone
No siblings
The pavements of Hanover
The walking dreamer
                    No bomb

No barbed wire
No aura of defeat

Escape to America!
Too late after the Holocaust
Etched into my brain

Always walking
Excited, with broken English
I was a wounded, mature
12-year-old
Unable to jump out of his skin
                    For you are

what you are

I constantly asked
How could
one percent of the population
Be such a hindrance?
Little time for love
For attention
                    Now, later

I do retain
Some of my religion
Always trying to visualize
The omnipotent God

Anxious to give love
Never learning how

With wild abandonment
I dug
new
roots

The Orphanage and the Train Ride Home

After the Auction occurred, I am sure I felt sad, but was not traumatized since too much else was going on. The warm love of my adopted Uncle and Aunt, and the news that I would be sent to an orphanage barely occupied my mind. All was so surreal.

Soon, my father reappeared with a passport, on his way to run a hotel in Rapallo with his brother and sister in Italy, on the Riviera, taking all the family money. Before he left, he took me on the six hour express train from Hanover to Stuttgart, then to Esslingen by cab to the hill above the Neckar river to the "Weisenhaus" Orphanage. The director was a brother of some friend in Hanover and I was added to the collection of some eighty or so youngsters, all aged 3 - 14. The building housed a small school, a synagogue and dining room, and upstairs were dormitories for all the children. Desperately homesick, I survived there for six months, learning to adapt. Finally a letter arrived stating that it was my turn to travel to America. This prompted one of the teachers to take me to the train which would take me, by myself, back to Hanover. It was a D-Zug (Express Train).I was excited to finally return home.

After the first stop on the train, I went outside on the platform for a ten minute break, looking at the people on the platform. Suddenly one civilian man, wearing a Hitler button, jumped on me;
"Bis du ein Jude?"
Of course, I said, "Yes".
"How dare you stick your tongue out at me?!"
I whimpered that I had done no such thing. He then pulled me into the train compartment, and called the police to have me arrested. The police questioned me for quite a while. I expressed my innocence, in tears, frightened. They then sealed off the compartment and the train left with me alone. At the next station, new police came on board and held up the huge train and interrogated me again. I repeated that I had never stuck my tongue out! The police finally left, and because of German laws, they decided to leave me in the compartment by myself for the rest of the journey. I sat by myself, scared to death. I was worried about what would happen to my mother. They might have punished her, even though I was innocent.

Four hours later I had to transfer to another train. German protocol demanded that I get my tickets back and my relieved mother received me in tears at my destination. As soon as I saw her I cried "Mother, something awful happened to me!"

The next morning we reported to the local police station, as was the law, but they were not aware of any issue, so the matter was closed. But I lived with the haunted, scared feeling for years, even after I came to the United States.

Holocaust Victim

Robbed of my childhood,
Bundled in smelly rags,
Humiliated to the lowest ebbs of Hell,
Stiffened with fright
Cannot distinguish day from night.

Swollen stomach, gnawing sickness,
Sunken, hollow eyes.
The heart beats,
Little hope.
Why survive? Why stay alive?

Like a beaten, degraded animal
That has felt man's inhumanity
To man,
Loved ones torn apart,
Castration, damnation.

How can other creatures
Partake in such ghastly features?
Maimed
Demonstrably scarred for life
I must survive! I must survive!
The heart beats.

There is little hope.

Boils, blood in the stool,
Bones tender and skinny,
Inflammation, degradation,
Broken shoes too tight
Famished, underweight

Will it end?
Will we transcend?
Will the will, the soul
Survive the disaster?
As assuredly it must.

We will not die,
We will not rot,
We do believe
We have a God
We painfully shout out loud,
Rehearse and curse.

Where are you, Master of the world?
Whose bleak, black hurricane unfurled?
Mournful, in pain
Return! Return, our gracious God,
And promise

Never again

Never again

366

The Kindertransport

When I was ten years old, in late 1935, I overheard Mutti saying, "I heard about a program where they send children overseas, without their parents, and place them in Jewish homes. Since Aunt Ilse went to Chicago in 1934, and also Grandfather Adolf's brother, who had come fifty years earlier, it sounds good. It is in Chicago, let me apply."

I was stuck, lonely, in school in the orphanage for six months before finally returning home, ready to go to America. But it was not yet to be! I waited month after month. We went to see the American Consul in Berlin who looked me over. Only 18 months later in August, 1938 with my little suitcase, at age 12, did I finally arrive in Hamburg.

Some 30 miles up the Elbe River, the ocean liner "Germany-New York" waited for me and I boarded with a chaperone and fourteen other youngsters. All this was a new adventure, and so exciting. I remember I loved to run around the aisles and the deck. I relished in the newly discovered fruit cocktail and other new dishes with great gusto. Most of all, I practiced my broken English which I had learned from a tutor (since I had not gone to formal school for the last one and a half years).

One day, during the nine day voyage, I descended one deck below, where the crew lived and worked. There on the wall, plastered for all to see, was the vicious, denigrating anti-Jewish newspaper, "Der Stuermer". I faced the Jewish cartoon and all its false lies and accusations, turned around, scared, and went quickly upstairs. No, I had not left the dark cloud of hate behind in Germany. I later found out that every second Kindertransport group had to go on a German liner, whereas Fred, my cousin, came on an American liner several months later, but not with the Kindertransport. He was seventeen and ended up working as a butcher.

Initially, in 1934, the Kindertransport planned to save 20,000 children aged 4 -16, but not enough Jewish homes nor money for their support, was available. Hilde, my cousin, came in 1935 and by 1939 and only four or five hundred kids in total were placed in the New York region, but later Texas, St. Louis, Chicago and even San Francisco joined in. All in all, about 1,200 – 1,400 were saved between 1934 - 1944.

It Never Happened

The green rolling meadow
Interspersed with foliage, trees
Casting an eerie shadow
Where starving women stumbled, would freeze
Anne Frank in youth enslaved, decayed
The British freed the living skeletons, too late.
My daughter Judy and I witnessed the gruesome mounds and tombs
5,000, 10,000 buried, then 5,000, 10,000 more, and more, and more
Among new blooms
Bergen-Belsen

IT NEVER HAPPENED

Remnants of French, Austrians and Germans interred
In southern Vichy, France
Uncle Karl, my father Siegfried, Uncle Walter all had earned
the Iron Cross – death, torture their reward – absurd
Prisoners of the SS and Himmler's plans
Disease, starvation, a year or so – Walter died
Siegfried, my dad, was shipped to Martinique
Uncle Karl, in a cattle car to Auschwitz in the night
Camp Gurs

IT NEVER HAPPENED

Steinheim, Westphalia
Weils, my family, rooted for hundreds of years
Orders to arrest 70-year-old Ida, grandmother, loyal matron
Innocent believer, part of 12 million tears
The ovens of Auschwitz her reward and patron
Old family farmhouse, family meadowland confiscated
Years later, I received $1,000 compensation
Auschwitz

IT NEVER HAPPENED

Some did escape with souls so jarred
Branded, naked, determined to rebuild
I, 12 years old, in Chicago spared
The anguish, pain of childhood now unfilled

But
I lived, I lived! I was 16 years old!
The death camps, the forced labor,
The continent under the thump of the master race
The ominous smell from burned flesh, gassed bodies
When it happened the world knew, but I was never told
Someone had to know? Where is man's conscience?
Cultured, civilized, reverted to the basest forms of bestiality

An orphan searching for identity
In a sea of freedom without life-savers
To carry cross and torch and memory and hurt
Remnant, rebuilt, grandchildren that thrive
In freedom

IT NEVER HAPPENED

I mourn the gypsies, disabled, protesters and priests
Nine million tortured, starved who died
I, angry, pained, stalked by those civilized beasts
Amongst them 1.5 million children – ghosts – few torturers tried

The children still live in my heart
I – you, invisible – seared
Could be the flame-branded number on our arm
Can't you see the child's wide and searching eyes?
How can we fathom such cruel, calculated extermination?

In God's name someone and heaven knew
Later: "We are sorry, we'll pay reparation"
How could the world stand by without a clue?
Pearl Harbor – defend freedom, save our nation
Incomprehensible – is it still happening?
I still can't understand, I still can't comprehend
I still can't   Can you?

Some say: "IT NEVER HAPPENED."

Memories of London

On a grimy, cold evening, after several weeks in a boat convoy, we landed in Liverpool, England. It was around September 1944, just after D-Day. As we carried our duffel bags off the gangplank, English women volunteers greeted us with warm tea.
"Would you like some milk?"
"No, thank you," we all answered, not yet being used to constant milk in tea as they did in England. It took only weeks of training in the Midlands (near Shrewsbury) that our tastes were modified with all the tea, milk and crumpets.

Our battalion of 800 was divided into three platoons, all of them Combat Engineers with a specialty of laying and picking up mine fields and, more importantly, building Bailey Bridges strong enough to run a lightweight tank across. Our platoons were readying for the famous Rhine crossing in Germany. To our sheer luck however, the Ramagen Bridge, one of the first, did not explode upon attack by the Germans, and was intact enough for our troops to cross in force. Other bridges similarly helped tens of thousands of armored troops to forge into Germany for the final rush late in 1944 and ending on May 6, 1945. Armistice was signed on May 7, 1945.

In England still, living in chilly Niessen huts (round metal barracks), we waited for our next tour of duty. A few hours leave gave us a chance to walk the streets of Shrewsbury, a quaint city of which I remember little. Several weeks later, with our half-ton trucks full of bridge equipment, we travelled to a region near Oxford to practice building bridges across the narrower section of the Thames River. Several times in October or November we were driven to the river, where we would unload the puzzle of a bridge, float part of it across to the opposite shore and from each side, unrolling it and fastening it in the middle. In the early afternoon a tank would trundle across and back and we'd then take the bridge apart in the cold, damp English weather. I don't remember a single sunny day in all those weeks.

On weekends, they drove us to a particular square in Oxford and let us loose to wander and explore the town's taverns and restaurants until we would all meet at 9PM in long lines at the designated pickup spot. The trucks would come and return us to our cold Niessen huts for the next week of bridge-building.

I never will forget one Sunday, as we reloaded the trucks to return to our barracks, eight or nine trucks arrived, with three of them filled with American Negro soldiers. Within seconds, the Southern "white boys" of our troop had begun heckling the "niggers" and calling them names, while the blacks retorted in turn. It was almost a repeat of the Civil War, the hatred, the unjust prejudice. "How on earth could this happen?" I asked myself. After all, we were all fighting the Nazis, on the same side! It was only years after this that General Eisenhower began racial integration in the United States. Naturally, having been born in Germany and experiencing prejudice directly, this bothered and hurt me especially, but I could do little, though the thought of such division bothered me for years.

Out of the 180 men in our battalion, there were only three Jews, but none ever experienced discrimination or negative comments that I knew of. I was regarded as German rather than Jewish. I was twelve when I first arrived in the United States and now, seven years later at the age of 19, was charged with giving one-hour orientation lessons to my company, recalling as much about Germany as I could, standing in the middle of a circle of my fellow soldiers. I also kept up-to-date with current news from the newspaper reports. I learned of the latest advances, and stuck a map with flags, showing the encirclement of Germany and the influence of Russia and Japan.

All was well on the Western Front, but then Hitler launched a pilotless plane with one ton of explosives, launched from somewhere in France, headed for London and other major cities.

"Ike, can you spare some troops?" Churchill supposedly asked Eisenhower. Since the British soldiers were scattered, fighting all over the world in India, Africa, Italy and even a northern flank near Holland, extra battalions were desperately needed to clean up the morning's wreckage and the havoc caused by these pilotless planes.

Several thousand of us, instead of heading for the front, were sent to the Han's Crescent Club, a hotel, where we stacked our rifles in the basement. For several days we walked the exciting London streets for the first time in our lives. Even with the blackout, we found our way to taverns, restaurants, shops and huge dance halls. After several days, the square block of nineteenth century buildings on Onslow Square was made available to

Royal Albert Hall, London
Dame Myra Hess concert

Training in Shrewsbury,
England

us, located two Tube stops away from Piccadilly Circus and one block from South Kensington station (the heart of the Tube in Central London).

Apparently Irish workers had lived there before us. The space was filled with a tremendous alcohol odor and it took us a week of scrubbing and cleaning to get the stench out, in order to inhabit the four floors of the long square block, with several thousand American soldiers ready to clean up the wreckage after bombings. Sure enough, five or ten bombs, usually at night, would rain down daily. Overhead, hundreds of huge balloons were ready to intercept the bombs, while English Spitfire pilots would chase them and often shoot them down before they could do damage. Soon the Germans retaliated to the balloons by putting blades in front of each bomber, in order to blow up the balloons upon impact. In all, several thousand such "V1" bombs were dropped.

Of course, many of the citizens slept in bomb shelters. The many Tube stations closed up around eleven PM, and people, families with blankets huddled by the tens of thousands down below until the morning trains ran again. Many stayed in bomb shelters in their own homes. One doctor showed me that he had a big steel cage in his home, big enough for four people, so even if the ceiling would cave in, he and his family slept safely, though very tight, in this cage at night. When bombs would hit, it was often the concussion along the streets, the rocks and secondary explosions that would do the most damage.

By December, Hitler's new weapon, the "V2", was launched.

This weapon was a rocket that was impossible to stop. Though there were no direct hits on Onslow Square, where we lived, ate and headquartered, we could still feel the earth shake when they hit anywhere nearby.

V1 rocket and launcher

and V2 rocket

All in all over 5,000 rockets were dropped. At one time, our battalion found eighty dead from one direct hit, and in those four months about 10,000 people were killed and over one million homes were damaged.

I never went in a shelter. We were young, and stupidly thought ourselves invincible. Our guard duty was to walk around a one block area, often with a rifle (and sometimes even a lady) at our side. We were free every evening, could go to the tavern and booze it up with the locals.

The Hammersmith was a huge dance hall that could fit thousands of dancers, not to mention a 30-piece orchestra, and two women for every uniformed man. There was also Covent Garden, the old Opera House where all the seats had been taken out, and two or three thousand people would come to dance, crushed in like sardines. Every second song the gals had the right to cut in, a marvel for a 20 year old like me, learning to dance. There was no alcohol here, but iced drinks of all kind, and people would sit in the upper boxes and look down on the mad, dancing crowd. I loved it, since I could walk there and take the Tube home, just two stations away and took only five minutes. For the Hammersmith dances, I had to take a bus both ways, often meeting joyous, good-looking English girls on the way, though I was not yet schooled in the art of wooing a maiden, but was happy with occasional hugs and kisses, and constantly afraid I might catch the clap, gonorrhea or all the stuff they warned us about. Some of the guys, of course, let their testosterone go berserk, later bragging about their conquests. Some of them were even married back home.

By January, the Battle of the Bulge demanded some of our soldiers to be sent to the Front as reserves. I wanted to go as an interpreter, to use my knowledge of German, but my Captain said, "Weil, we need you when we get to the continent! You are the only one who is truly fluent in German!"

Sometime in March 1945, a convoy of trucks went to the southern cliffs on the English Channel to board ships that were part of a huge convoy, carrying thousands of troops simultaneously to Cherbourg, France. Just before boarding, an Englishman threw me a 6-8 page daily newspaper which read, "Hanover bombed for the third day!" How ironic; my home town, completely levelled by our bombers.

Many patrol boats and other military ships surrounded our convoy as it left after dark. The water was extremely rough. From time to time we could hear the depth charges sent to dissuade the German submarines which were on the prowl. At daylight we disembarked on to a half-ton truck. I could see the whole old city levelled, not a building was standing. This bombing was actually done by the us, the allies, before invading France. A track had been cleared through the debris for our trucks to head out to the tent city near Rouen called "Lucky Strike."

I did act as interpreter and supervised German PW's as they dug large holes the size of graves, to build our own sewage system. I did this by intuition, only to find, twenty years later, that this is how feces settle into the earth and local farmers benefited later by using the rich "fertilizer" on their fields!

"They need a clerk back at Lucky Strike, France! Weil, you go, temporarily!"

They typed out an order to the new commander for me to travel by train via Paris. As a military person I could travel for free on any train. I had earlier visited my mother's three cousins in Brussels who, as Jews, were hidden by a French woman for four years.

Once I got off the train in Paris with my duffel bag and mere clothes (and almost broke,) I made a crucial decision. Why go directly to Rouen and then to work as clerk-typist at Lucky Strike? There was a Red Cross Club here in Paris where I could bunk for free. I could buy a carton (10 packs) of cigarettes, daily and did ($2.00 per pack, but only my five cents to me). So I got "lost" in Paris: I heard a concert by the Violinist Heifetz, I saw the great sights, went out to Versailles, looked for SHAEF Headquarters (it was gone, moved the Rheims, I found out later). I had my picture taken in front of Sacré Coeur, then and again in 1992, forty-six years later!

Arthur Weil at Lucky Strike, 1945

Exhausted, I took the train the Rouen, where a truck picked me up and brought me to Lucky Strike.
"Where have you been?" one of the sergeants inquired, seeing my paper stamped 25 times. I kept my mouth shut, grinned and said nothing.

Our job was to do mimeographs, since 50,000 American soldiers (who had been prisoners of war, many of which were pilots and officers) were interrogated before being sent back home. Many were mistreated by the Germans, who experienced great shortages at the end of the war. They had been starved but after a week they would say, "Oh, as prisoners, it wasn't so bad!" It is amazing how memory changes at times.

My stay for several weeks was uneventful. When it was time to return, again I took the train from Rouen, and again I got lost in Paris for a week. I finally returned to my outfit, the 1284th Combat Engineer battalion. A week later, we took the train back, believe it or not, back to Lucky Strike for the third time and then finally home. The war against Japan was still on and our mission was "to San Francisco and then the Far East."

"No way, Jose!" I said to myself, but that is another story.

I am Every Man

My mind and body
Span the continent
In every shape and color I am every man
I till the soil, excavate minerals
Clear debris, create metropolises
A combustion of man's creativity
I am every man

I announce myself, the exquisite inventor
Mixer of chemicals and potions
Create magic boxes
Vials, bottles which hold mysterious rays

Communicate within the unending universe
Fantasize, philosophize, idealize
Inventor, builder and destroyer
I am everyman

Mesmerized by my own reflection
I shape realms, safeguard with an enchanted will
And, with human folly, climb moonbeams
Only to recover on the sordid muddy soil

I am tossed like a nutshell in a pond
Rising and blown by breezes like a balloon
I am there, helpless, to observe and scan all
Until the sole of my shoe touches ground again

I, you, we
Build frames of tradition and truth
Or destroy with unseeing anger
Led by demagogues of technology and false religion

Blinded, duped, consumed with passion and hate
With a perspective, walled in by the cement of ignorance
Collective man's colossus rises
Asserts and drowns in his own abundance

Be he heathen or bigot
The demon and demanding chemicals of the brain
And all the philosophers' warnings are cast aside
Until, too soon, the last bell rings

And I see the end of an ignorant generation
In self-destruction,
And they thirst no more
Leaving to the next to re-build and repair

While some Holy spirit hovers to regenerate
Recoup both good and bad
You have a soul!
Who will ever know that the heart beats on
Then the heart stops and the spirit passes

I am everyman

Neat suit, neat shoes and freckles galore
Had lunch but found him an awful bore
So proper, so prim, so neat
So dull and uninformed, I do repeat

Life's rat race should have some mice too...

Life often is a comedy of errors
With laughter and frivolity.
Hopefully no tragic ending
Nor big bills to pay later

There was a time

There was a time when elections mattered
Old and new immigrants accepted scattered
Hope for our country was paramount
With happy business now all around

    (Not gangs and shoot-outs all around)

    There was a time of peace and rest
    Where hope, prosperity were blessed
    We lived in dignity, respect, routine
    Drive-by shootings never seen

There was a time of courtship, sweet
When banana splits were one great treat
Where after many dates you'd steal a kiss
In safety of your family all full of bliss

    (Not gangs and shoot-outs all around)

    There was a time where all did work
    Be it janitor, teacher, driver, clerk
    And human dignity ranked high
    No deadly shot disturbed with a drive-by

There was a time of hope and prayer
Where neighbors helped and all did
care
In nature's beauty picked own fruit
Only hunters were out to shoot

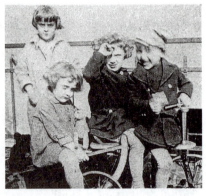

(Not gangs and shoot-outs all around)

There was a time of faith
Of manners, attitudes and grace
Where love and marriage lasted
And honor, friendships not out-casted

(Not gangs and shoot-outs all around).

The Photographer

A foolish funny foible and big fault
For my photographic skills soon called
My hobby photographs amass
For entertaining they do really pass
But do not be annoyed
My sayings and writings are not yet destroyed

Instead my camera keeps prizewinning pictures galore
I could kiss, accolades and I could score
Or fall flat on my face or drown
Or simply leave this town
But where to share, where to show
I have the talent, where to go?

To dig new roots and make new friend
Someone that my fixation will soon understand
Pictures of some minutia or colossal feat
The character within the picture you soon meet
And with this magic art at hand
I'll join the unique artistic band

And though off tune I'll sing my song
For now at length I know where I belong

My memory lately is half bad
It's the other half that worries me.

**The recently freed concentration camp (and other) prisoners
slowly re-establish themselves and survive as Displaced Persons.**
A footnote to history!

This is a true historical account, seldom related. With little imagination it hits your guts.

It was a callous, cruel world, yet I was lucky in June 1945, I survived World War II as an American soldier. Later, in May 1945, I was stationed as a combat engineer running supplies for ten million people, from the Meuse River, Liege in Belgium. We were attached to SHAEF (Allied Expeditionary Forces) and had the insignia patch on our uniforms. As a twenty year-old Jew, even I was blind to the extent of the Holocaust and its inhumane consequences, soon to become so evident.

Much of my own family (grandmother, uncles, cousins) had perished in the concentration camps and ovens, I discovered later. I could not fathom the enormity of this greatest of crimes against a small innocent group.

Now, seventy years later, to my dismay and chagrin, with anger, guilt and sadness, I learn about the aftermath of 1945, when emaciated, crippled, sick prisoners (many Jewish) were freed from the camps. Jewish children who had been sheltered and hidden in convents and with private families, were now freed and let loose into an unknown world, an excess of over 30,000 Jewish kids.

All the while I learn these facts, I was imagining, I could easily have been one of those lucky survivors. One and half million innocent Jewish children were ruthlessly eradicated from this earth during the Holocaust (1940-1945).You can't blame the two million displaced persons in 1945 from not wanting to go home, to poor untenable conditions, for example to Communist Russia or in case of many of the Jews, Germany, Poland, Ukraine, Rumania, and other parts of Eastern Europe. Those home countries were now a cemetery for them. They were hated, not wanted, not accepted, in peril and could not risk returning, despite the horrors of temporary survival. Now, like prisoners still, they had to live in Displaced Persons ("DP") camps under guard all over Europe. At this stage, in 1945, few countries would admit this stateless humanity. They were treated as if they were under the old Nazi German supervision!

President Harry S. Truman sent Earl G. Harrison, Dean of the University of Pennsylvania Law School, to investigate. He reported back on the shocking conditions. "As things stand now, we appear to be treating the Jews as the Nazis treated them, except that we do not exterminate them," (Summer '45). Soon, Truman and General Eisenhower implemented better conditions for the DP's in Germany and Italy. The DP camps in Italy and Southern France were more hopeful, for these were deportation ports to Palestine and elsewhere. Soon, the Jews were treated as a special ethnic group, put into Jewish camps, meeting their needs. They enjoyed a degree of autonomy. Agencies of the United Nations, United States, Britain and particularly Jews from Palestine came to help. The Nuremberg Trial exposed more of the brutal systematic eradication of all Jews.

An illegal organized mass movement called "B'richa" was born. The dilemma was that the US and other major world countries refused Jews to emigrate, still keeping them incarcerated and homeless. There were a total of 1,200,000 or more displaced, stateless, and homeless. 80% were Christian, but 20% (about 250,000) were Jewish survivors. Can you imagine, months later (not until 1947-48) were serious efforts made to empty the camps.The "Mossad Le'Aliyah Bet" group, amongst others, sent missionaries in 1945 to rescue and organize a Jewish exodus on a large scale. They provided false documents, food, shelter and transportation to town, moving thousands of newly-freed Jews across the Alps and Tatra mountains, often carrying the children and elderly. No one got paid. All were volunteers. This undercover operation was also aided by Jewish volunteers from the Jewish Brigade of Palestine, which provided trucks and provisions to transport tens of thousands of people. Secretly, the American Distribution Committee and other organizations helped the holocaust survivors. By 1947, 30,000 children were still waiting to go to Israel, the most common destination for most Jews. These children were gathered in 130 homes in 13 countries. It is hard to believe that 500 children alone survived in Buchenwald, 100 in Auschwitz and 10,000 Hungarians waited for the Aliyah. Only 68,000 Jews were released from monasteries, churches and private homes where they were hidden from the Nazis, with chains and crosses hanging around their necks. The Habesha operated from fifty centers in ten European countries, aided by 150 representatives and 350 holocaust survivors.

Between January 1, 1949 and December 31, 1952, over 400,000 displaced persons entered the United States, which included many Jews. Why did it take so much time for the US to allow them in, when by 1948-1949 Israel alone had saved
over 167,000 of their own people? It was prejudice, lack of leadership from the White House, and congressional procrastination that prolonged the ordeal of the survivors. Was this a "Schande," (disgrace); a secondary crime against a defenseless, creative, good people?

I must remind you that these poor (yet lucky!) newcomers were patient and sweated hard for years before reaping successful results. Many also went to Australia, New Zealand, Mexico and South Africa.

By 1953, after more than eight years after liberation, 170,000 DPs had entered Israel where many tens of thousands still survive today, including some distant relatives of mine. These are but statistics. I can only imagine the struggle and fortitude of survival.   *Amen!*

Today, Here and Now

Now, in 2014, at the age of eighty-eight, I am truly excited with my life. Twice a week I venture out to see plays, symphonies, operas, orchestras, lectures etc. I still manage two apartment buildings, write my poetry and essays, fool around with stocks daily, watch too much TV, and enjoy my family and significant other.

My house is like a hermit's heaven; full of books, a mismatch of innocuous oil paintings, photographs of family and a dozen boxes of my twenty poetry books, ready to give out for free. With my ultra-modern kitchen I enjoy cooking and I grow tomatoes, strawberries and pick my oranges and lemons every year. I am surrounded by beautiful trees and homes, and we enjoy a most fantastic climate, ten minutes from the University of California, Berkeley.

I happily breathe fresh, free air and enjoy 360 days of Northern California sunshine.

Grandson Josh

Jordan, Jeff and Madison

Madison and her dog, Bella

My daughter Judy, son Jeff, grandson Jordan and myself.

My four grandkids; Ben, Madison, Josh and Jordan and myself.

Imagine 88

Imagine you made it to eighty-eight
Twilight year so weighty
Spectacular life, now history
The precious days and months ahead, a mystery
Imagine 88

Amazing, I survive, still tested
All stages of life, now bested
Rare, good friends are my concern
Wish my grandkids long life, always learn
Imagine 88

Still pour out my heart and soul
Hurt, the pain will heal, now whole
In our cosmos we are but a tiny speck
Life's secret treasured, always on attack
Imagine 88

Still hours left to celebrate
Amuse, dance and stay up late
Embrace my friends and charm
Wish you love and joy and never harm
Imagine 88

I look now at my weathered, aged face
Endured and celebrated a lifelong race
Amazing that my old body still can cope
Desirous libido full of innocence and hope
Imagine 88

The beauty of nature is still mine selective
The taste of touch, sound and smell elective
Search, feel, taste, sense in a world alone
All are rapture, for mistakes I do atone
Imagine 88

It's lucky that we really do not know
Tomorrow's heartache or surprising show
This gift of life surprise is granted to us every day
Thank you, I'll take it, and I'll toast you all and say
Imagine 88

I'll say thanks and graciously I share
Love you in friendship and I care
May you prosper, in best of health
Remember, in life your happiness is still the greatest wealth
Imagine 88

If you can laugh while you're dying, you know
you made it!

Rejoice, with an
infusion of spirited
admiration

Stand, raise your arms
Halleluiah!
Try to brace yourself
and stay uplifted

For blessed are the
meek!

Wisdom Tree

This is no time to shake my wisdom tree
As caterpillar-eaten curled leaves flutter to the sidewalk
And stale, dull opinions are uselessly peppered
Is life exciting, a bitch or a teeter-totter
Up and down, and in between?
Each day of my older age brings a miracle
                        of cures and discoveries
Of joy, of pain, of suffering sprinkled with hope
Better yet, momentary surprise or shock

Nibble, chew, touch, as if you could freeze the good man
Discard the aches, look only at his rich past life
Jumping into the car to a new adventure
Or simply hold the moment, hold something
Reclining with an open book
Pleading for 10 more exciting pages
Five more delightful nights
Or simply minutes, packed with impressions
All local, direct, intimate and revealing

If I could buy time I would
spend it all
Cautious, selective, mindful!

Arthur and wife, Lillian, 1954

Measure my advances
In life we all take chances
Dare strike a nerve
The family and name pre-
serve
Our imagination into truthful
act
Self-sealed our goal with
much respect

Age reflection

Slowly, deliberately, his rich, filled day
Adventure, gray, silvery hairs
Like a grazing cow chewing eagerly
Body moves consciously, rhythmically
Aching back, arthritic fingers
Still, the vital spirit so vibrant
Timeline, months do tick, tenaciously hanging on
Like a sentence, ignoring the clock of reality

    Will the curtain come down suddenly, too soon?
    Damn time, birthdays zoom
    Each meal, each laugh, a gift
    Dare not jinx a good thing
    Satiable, alert, still want to close loopholes

        New gadgets, inventions, Facebook, Google
        Overwhelming, mind-blowing
        Still discover the mystery
        The interrelationship of the universe

Still time for tender passion, for all kinds of love
The old guy moves in his own smiling orbit
Of kindness, and affection helping others
He greets with a skinny outstretched arm
He didn't reveal advanced prostrate cancer
A grand tour of his life in retrospect instead

    Memories so lifelike spring out
    From photo albums and old movies
    Relive, imagine, recall and revel in my inner sanctum
    Maybe a few months more, or even a year or two

        Precious days left, days of awe and wonder
        Always the certain common denominators
        Love, touch, embrace — hold on only to let go
        Pry open an ever-eager heart
        So much more to do, to see

Yet time and heart tick on
Too busy to give them much thought
Always, while there is still time!
It's now I smile, and touch, and kiss, embrace
Tomorrow or ten years hence may be my last day.

Just a reminder that good effort pays off!

Did you hug a dear one today?
Did you feed a dog, cat, horse or fish?
Did you give a compliment, a good word to someone?
Did you speak up against some unfairness in your home, family, neighborhood or politician's action?
Did you take personal time off to think, pray, wake up and assess your inner self?
Did you read something?
Did you read a bit of poetry?
Did you clean up part of your room or house or car?
Did you do an act of charity?
Did you brush your teeth, shower and keep up your personal hygiene?

≈ ≈ ≈

An Author's Sigh

This book may someday be valuable,
Or it may sit on the shelf,
Sold at a flea market for 10 cents
Soon to be recycled.

You see me!
If. really me!
Wil
To Arthur Weil
Best Wishes, Joe Loom art '99

Can't you save me?
Share me?

ML   7-14